Tales of Human Frailty and the Gentleness of God

Tales of Human Frailty and the Gentleness of God

Kenneth G. Phifer

JOHN KNOX PRESS
ATLANTA, GEORGIA

Library of Congress Cataloging in Publication Data
Phifer, Kenneth G
    Tales of human frailty and the gentleness of God.

    Includes bibliographical references.
    1. Bible stories, English—O. T.   I. Title.
BS550.2.P48   221.9'505   73-16914
ISBN 0-8042-2197-9

Contents

To the memory of my father,
who taught me to love
the people and the stories
of the Bible.

Introduction

Once upon a time Elie Wiesel, author and teacher, spoke in New Orleans at our nearby Jewish Community Center. It was a ghastly night—raining so hard that you sloshed as you walked, the wind blowing so that you clung frantically to your umbrella, which threatened to blow away and carry you with it. One of my sons and I went to hear the lecture, parking three blocks away, and fighting the wind and the rain to sit in a corner of a jam-packed auditorium.

Elie Wiesel. Who is he? A voice from the "Holocaust," as he calls the Hitler years in Europe, an authentic witness to the agony of the Jewish people. He spent his adolescent years in Auschwitz and Buchenwald. For ten years, after his release in 1945, he refrained from writing, feeling that the "Holocaust" was something to be absorbed, to be brooded over, to fight back from for sanity. Then, after ten years, he began to tell his story, the story of his people. Now, more than twenty-five years later, he still tells stories, insisting that mankind lives by the stories that it tells; that it passes on wisdom from generation to generation by stories. More, men find out who they are by the stories that are told them, the stories that they pass on to their children. The stories need not be true in the sense that they are factual, as two and two make four, but in the sense that they say something true about God and man and the meaning of life. They must be true in the sense that they help us identify who we are and what we believe about our universe.

Storytelling is more than an idle pastime. In an issue of *Saturday Review,* critic Malcolm Cowley lamented the loss of storytelling by modern writers. Now novelists reject plot "in favor of 'immediacy,' that is, of plunging the reader into . . . a welter of

sense impressions." [1] Perhaps as much as anything else, the loss
of the ability to tell a story symbolizes a loss of faith, a loss of a
sense of direction and flow in life, of self-identity. Elie Wiesel
prefaces his novel *The Gates of the Forest* with a story, a parable.

> When the great Rabbi Israel Baal Shem-Tov saw misfortune
> threatening the Jews it was his custom to go into a certain part
> of the forest to meditate. There he would light a fire, say a
> special prayer, and the miracle would be accomplished and the
> misfortune averted.
>
> Later, when his disciple, the celebrated Magid of Mezritch,
> had had occasion, for the same reason, to intercede with heaven,
> he would go to the same place in the forest and say: "Master of
> the Universe, listen! I do not know how to light the fire, but I
> am still able to say the prayer." And again the miracle would
> be accomplished.
>
> Then it fell to Rabbi Israel of Rizhyn to overcome mis-
> fortune. Sitting in his armchair, his head in his hands, he
> spoke to God: "I am unable to light the fire and I do not know
> the prayer; I cannot even find the place in the forest. All I can
> do is to tell the story, and this must be sufficient." And it was
> sufficient. [2]

Wiesel intends this as a parable of our world, where many
men are unable to light the fire, do not know the words of prayer,
cannot even find the place of worship. It is a parable of a world
of emptiness and uncertainty, of "children at the gate/Who will
not go away and cannot pray." [3] To all such, we must keep alive
the memory of the stories. Are you aware that the Bible is primarily a book of stories? Remember the hymn that goes "Tell
me the old, old story of Jesus and his love"? How long since
you've heard a story, a real story?

The stories told in this book are ancient. They are all tales
told long ago. They survived because they were and are so real.
In each of them there is a man or a woman who is living out
some experience so closely akin to our experience that we can
identify ourselves if we look hard enough. For each of us is in
motion in life, swinging between grace and gracelessness. Sometimes we hide as Adam and Eve hid. Sometimes we run as Cain
ran and as Jonah ran. Sometimes we are restless, searching,

questing, as Abraham was, leaving the familiar for the unknown. But all the time our gracelessness is surrounded by the grace of God, for the grace of God is the healing wholeness of being. It is the sense of being found when we are hiding. It is the touch of a Presence while we are on the run. It is a finger pointing toward a sheltered place in a storm. It is a feeling that Someone is there when we are lonely. It is so indescribable that we cannot put it into the framework of our words and thoughts. We can only tell tales of the way it operates. We can only say, "Look, that is how it is."

So these tales are told of our gracelessness and God's grace. In every case the grace is greater than the gracelessness, the tenderness overwhelms the awkardness.

> I say that we are wound
> With mercy round and round
> As if with air.[4]

A Tale of Peril and Promise

Once upon a time there was a man named Adam and a woman named Eve. So the story goes in the book of Genesis, that Biblical book of beginnings. We really ought not to smile about Adam and Eve and toss off their story as though it were just another story, a pre-scientific effort to explain the origins of the universe. We ought not to feel superior or to laugh because our old editions of the King James Version of the Bible solemnly record in the margin that the creation took place in the year 4004 B. C. This chronology is based upon the work of one James Ussher, Anglican Archbishop of Armagh in Ireland, who calculated it exactly: "at the beginning of the night before Monday, the 23rd of October, 4004 B.C." [1]

So, you believe that you know better. You know that the universe is millions upon millions of years old. You know that the origins of man are lost in dim prehistory. But what do you know that is more important than these words?

> In the beginning God created the heavens and the earth. The earth was without form and void, and darkness was upon the face of the deep; and the spirit of God was moving over the face of the waters. . . .
> Then God said, "Let us make man in our image, after our likeness . . ." So God created man in his own image, in the image of God he created him; male and female he created them.[2]

A problem that arises for many people is the point of a conflict between evolution and creation. But such a conflict is an artificial problem, due primarily to a misuse of the Bible, combined with a misunderstanding of what science really is.

Once upon a time there was a man named Adam and a woman named Eve, so the Biblical story goes. And that story contains a view of the world and of God that is the most important thing that we can possibly know about it. Of course, the physical origins of the universe are lost in prehistory. Of course, the world is millions upon millions of years old. Of course, there has been a long, slow, labored process from the organic scum to the Mona Lisa. Biology is one way of telling about that process in our world. The story of Adam and Eve is another way of telling the same thing. If we lose what their story represents, we may lose the most important truth about our world. For we will lose the framework within which both the organic scum and the Mona Lisa fit at last. Then the biological story does not matter very much.

There are two creation stories in the early chapters of Genesis. In the first of these stories it is recorded: "God created man in his own image." [3] In the second it is recorded: ". . . the LORD God formed man of dust from the ground, and breathed into his nostrils the breath of life; and man became a living being." [4] The word translated "man," meaning human in a generic sense, is the Hebrew word "a-dam," which later was transliterated into the proper noun "Adam." So in the Genesis stories, "a-dam," "Adam," is Man, a human being. The symbolism, however, of that reality is lost if Adam is confined to a solitary individual or limited to a male figure. He is you! He is me! His story is retold in the lives of us all. He and we are curious creations made in the image of God from the dust of the ground.

His story and our story is one of kinship with the earth, of our belonging in our world. Never forget that Adam is "of the ground." He belongs to nature. He fits his surroundings. He is of the earth, earthy. In the first chapter of Genesis, after each stage of creation, there is that recurring phrase, "And God saw that it was good." After all else was done, "God created man in his own image. . . . God saw everything that he had made, and behold, it was very good." [5] The world God made is interrelated. It is one. And the man he made is a part of that creation. Earth is our mother. Out of the womb of Earth we come.

Yet, the man Adam was apart from earth also. The story of Adam is the story of belonging and of longing. Who is this "stalemate of dust and desire"? asks Faulkner. Is he but another animal? In the very asking of the question we imply the answer. What other animal examines himself and judges himself? What other animal aspires and longs? What other animal asks questions of the universe? "Man is the only animal that laughs and weeps, since he alone perceives the difference between things as they are and as they ought to be."[6]

Like us, the figure called Adam aspired and wept and reached and felt that he was free. And still Adam aspires and still he weeps and still he wants to be free.

Now, the importance of all of this for us in our age is incalculable. If we are creatures, nonetheless we are creatures whose sense of who we are is stretched out to embrace infinity. Paradoxically, however, we live in an age in which man is often denigrated. We even denigrate ourselves. We feel that we are graceless.

We have lived through Dachau and Buchenwald and Nuremberg and My Lai. We have lost our innocence and, with our lost innocence, we have lost our illusions. We have come down to bedrock about ourselves. There is nothing we will not do, no sin, no cruelty of which humans are not capable at one time or another.

Once there was a person called Adam. Everyman! He sang and he sinned. Even as you and I. He wept and he wondered. He dreamed and he doubted. He made promises and broke them. Dust and stars, shade and sunlight. Fearfully and wonderfully made. Even as you and I.

And then, there was Eve. Perhaps here the most significant thing about mankind emerges. For man not only reaches toward God as he prays and as he sings; he reaches out toward others in love. Once there was Adam, and then there was Eve, and the story is told in the book of Genesis. It is a beautiful tale of a pristine garden. How meaningful this garden picture must have been to the desert nomads among whom the story was first told. Their lives were bounded by the arid sands of the desert. They lived amid a primeval emptiness. An oasis, when one was sighted, was a miracle for them, a miracle where life and refreshment awaited them and their flocks. No wonder some desert poet's imagination pictured God creating a garden and saw the bubbling springs, the budding trees, and the singing grass, and amid all that beauty, a man and a woman dwelling. The Lord God himself came down to walk in the garden in the cool of an evening.

It is the tale of a simple and direct relationship—man close to God. If God once had thought, "I'm lonely; I'll make me a man," then he thought also, "Man is lonely; I'll make him a companion."

> So the LORD God caused a deep sleep to fall upon the man, and while he slept took one of his ribs and closed up its place with flesh; and the rib which the LORD God had taken from the man he made into a woman and brought her to the man. Then the man said,
> "This at last is bone of my bones
>   and flesh of my flesh;
> she shall be called Woman,
>   because she was taken out of Man."
> Therefore a man leaves his father and his mother and cleaves to his wife, and they become one flesh.[7]

It is a tale of innocence. Sex was unselfconscious, untainted by furtiveness.

> And the man and his wife were both naked, and were not ashamed.[8]

It is a tale of a tree, a mysterious tree. Tradition has identified it as an apple tree. But there is nothing in the story to indicate what kind of a tree it was except that it was a mysterious tree, bearing the fruit of life itself—and that strange command.

> The LORD God took the man and put him in the garden of Eden to till it and keep it. And the LORD God commanded the man, saying, "You may freely eat of every tree of the garden; but of the tree of the knowledge of good and evil you shall not eat, for in the day that you eat of it you shall die."[9]

This is a tale with a darker side. It is a tale of corruption, a tale that features the first snake in the grass in history.

> Now the serpent was more subtle than any other wild crea-

ture that the LORD God had made. He said to the woman, "Did God say, 'You shall not eat of any tree of the garden'?" And the woman said to the serpent, "We may eat of the fruit of the trees of the garden; but God said, 'You shall not eat of the fruit of the tree which is in the midst of the garden, neither shall you touch it, lest you die.' " But the serpent said to the woman, "You will not die. For God knows that when you eat of it your eyes will be opened, and you will be like God, knowing good and evil." So when the woman saw that the tree was good for food, and that it was a delight to the eyes, and that the tree was to be desired to make one wise, she took of its fruit and ate; and she also gave some to her husband, and he ate.[10]

It is a tale of disobedience and lost innocence.

Then the eyes of both were opened, and they knew that they were naked; and they sewed fig leaves together and made themselves aprons.[11]

It is a tale of human shiftiness, the first illustration of a finger pointing to evade personal responsibility and to say, "It's his fault."

And they heard the sound of the LORD God walking in the garden in the cool of the day, and the man and his wife hid themselves from the presence of the LORD God among the trees of the garden. But the LORD God called to the man, and said to him, "Where are you?" And he said, "I heard the sound of thee in the garden, and I was afraid, because I was naked; and I hid myself." He said, "Who told you that you were naked? Have you eaten of the tree of which I commanded you not to eat?" The man said, "The woman whom thou gavest to be with me, she gave me fruit of the tree, and I ate." Then the LORD God said to the woman, "What is this that you have done?" The woman said, "The serpent beguiled me, and I ate." [12]

And so it is a tale with an unhappy ending.

... therefore the LORD God sent him forth from the garden of Eden, to till the ground from which he was taken. He drove out the man; and at the east of the garden of Eden he placed the cherubim, and a flaming sword which turned every way, to guard the way to the tree of life. [13]

Quite a story! A whole series of pictures—not explanations, mind you. Whence came evil? The story does not say. What is the nature of this tree of "the knowledge of good and evil"? The story does not say. And what does it mean to us? Has this ancient attempt to grapple with the origins of evil and sin, estrangement and alienation, nothing to say to us? Is not this scene an eternal happening, a timeless tale, always so, regardless of the changes in the world around us? Is it not a story continuously reenacted, behind twentieth-century faces, by people who hide their nakedness in twentieth-century fashion? We are all, in one way or another, Adam and Eve.

People still make their choices. The Pope, in Browning's *The Ring and the Book,* has it: "Life's business being just the terrible choice." Adam and Eve started it, the whole business of falling from God's grace-filled creation, the whole business of disobedience and furtiveness and evasion. But we carry it on. That is our problem when we get down to basics. The tale of Adam and Eve is a tale of the choice, as our lives are tales of choices, choices that are often not clear-cut and plain. Life's perils and promises intermingle. Good and evil intermesh until at times they are almost indistinguishable. Comedy and tragedy shade into one another. But the choices, the terrible choices, are the very nature of man.

There was Adam and there was Eve, and they chose. And their tale is a tale of woeful consequences. It is a tale of pride and the results of pride. "Did God say?" the serpent asked Eve. There is the question. Did God say, did he really say, "Thou shalt and thou shalt not"? Did he really say, "You are mine. I made you and I have formed you. You cannot be your own God"? Did God say? And Eve listened and fondled the question, even as we all do. She listened again, and the tempter whispered once more, "Did God say? Hah! You shall not die. You are free to be your own God, free to forget your creaturehood. You, too, are creators." So we all eventually believe it to be true.

And still the tale unfolds. "Did God say?" The whisper comes to each of us in some form or other. Did God say to me, "Thou shalt and thou shalt not," or am I not exempt? Am I not my own, able to discern for myself my own good and evil?

Each of us falls from innocence. "How man fell, I admit I

do not know; why he fell, I now know within my own self," confessed Soren Kierkegaard. This is the meaning of the story of Adam and Eve. When the Fall becomes an aspect of *my* history, *my* moments in time, then I really see who Adam and Eve are.

For our lost innocence is, at last, our severed relationships in life. "The eyes of both were opened, and they knew that they were naked," [14] and they were ashamed. What does this mean but that now they had so attempted to achieve their own desires that they had grown apart from one another, each bearing the burden of suspicion of the other, each bearing estrangement? There was a new and terrible loneliness for them.

This story, then, represents the introduction of distrust and alienation between man and fellowman, man and God. For the evening came and the Lord God walked in the garden. Adam and Eve hid themselves in the trees of the garden. And we are still hiding from each other and from God.

So, on weary feet, Adam and Eve stumble through time and come to life again in you and me. This is the whole human epic in epitome. It is what the Bible is about. It is what the book of Genesis is about—not about a time when a man and a woman suddenly began to speak Hebrew and cultivate roses. No, what one meets in the Creation stories is the truth about oneself, a truth that speaks directly to oneself, and sets a person to nodding his head and saying, "Yes! Yes, I recognize that." The road to the garden of Eden is traced through the human heart. We know Adam and Eve. We recognize that garden where we, too, have dreamed of innocence. We have talked with the serpent. Worse! We have listened as he asked insidiously, "Did God say?" We have eaten of the tree of the knowledge of good and evil. We have seen the angel with his flaming sword, and we know that we cannot dwell in Eden. We have wandered where the wild thorns and wild thistles grow, where there are none but wild plants to eat. Like Franz Kafka, we say "Sometimes I feel I understand the Fall of Man better than anyone."

But that is not all.

And they heard the sound of the LORD God walking in

the garden in the cool of the day, and the man and his wife hid themselves from the presence of the LORD God among the trees of the garden. But the LORD God called to the man, and said to him, "Where are you?"[15]

"Where are you?" All of life, says Kyle Haselden, is a tale of peril and promise, and the active agents between the peril and the promise lead us to the one or to the other, to the peril or the promise. And that is what the Bible is about.

It is said that in the early church the cross was often flanked with an apple (one end of time) and a trumpet (the other end of time), the apple representing the peril of human choices, the trumpet representing the promise of triumph through the Spirit of God, and the cross in the midst, the agent of redemption.

Where are you? Where are you? This gentle voice calls in the cool of the evening. And we who are both Adam and Eve, hiding in the trees, trying to cover our nakedness and our human frailty with fig leaves, are haunted by the voice, for it has never quit calling. Where are you?

Sins Too Big for God?

Once upon a time there were brothers. One was named Cain and one was named Abel. Their tale is a dark tale of brooding jealousy, a story told by thickened tongues of blood crying out from the ground. Cain and Abel! It is a haunting tale of passion and treachery and, ultimately, of fratricide; a mournful tale of remorse, wild regret, banishment. It is one of the oldest tales in all of literature, one most highly charged with basic human emotions. It may even be interpreted as a pre-Freudian tale of sibling rivalry, of two sons seeking the father's blessing. One of them felt the father's blessing was received, the other knew only the barrenness of rejection. And out of it all flamed tragedy and death.

John Steinbeck constructed his novel *East of Eden* around the Adam-Eve, Cain-Abel theme. In one scene, Samuel speaks to Lee, the Chinese cook:

> "Two stories have haunted us and followed us from our beginning," Samuel said. "We carry them along with us like invisible tails—the story of original sin and the story of Cain and Abel. And I don't understand either of them. I don't understand them at all but I feel them. Liza gets angry with me. She says I should not try to understand them. She says why should we try to explain a verity. Maybe she's right—maybe she's right. Lee, Liza says you're a Presbyterian—do you understand the Garden of Eden and Cain and Abel?" . . .
>
> "I think I understand the Fall. I could perhaps feel that in myself. But the brother murder—no. Well, maybe, I don't remember the details very well." [1]

The brother murder—we do not understand at all! Or do we, deep down, really understand better than we admit? We do not like to remember the details at all. They may be too intimate, become too personal. Do you not feel the shiver of identification when they are recalled to you?

In the Hebrew account of the dim beginning of things, after Adam and Eve were expelled from the Garden of Eden, it is recorded:

> Now Adam knew Eve his wife, and she conceived and bore Cain, saying, "I have gotten a man with the help of the LORD." And again, she bore his brother Abel. Now Abel was a keeper of sheep, and Cain a tiller of the ground. In the course of time Cain brought to the LORD an offering of the fruit of the ground, and Abel brought of the firstlings of his flock and of their fat portions. And the LORD had regard for Abel and his offering, but for Cain and his offering he had no regard. So Cain was very angry, and his countenance fell. . . . Cain said to Abel his brother, "Let us go out to the field." And when they were in the field, Cain rose up against his brother Abel, and killed him.[2]

This is the story of the first murder! Walter Russell Bowie points out: ". . . there is no indication that Cain intended to commit murder. . . . Cain strikes Abel in the instinctive reflex of his anger, but who can say that he had any deliberate purpose to end his brother's life? When Abel fell Cain may have been astonished that he lay so long, so still. Why did he not get up again? Only little by little, and incredulously, did Cain grow conscious that something had happened beyond the framework of his previous imagining. This motionless body on the ground that did not speak or stir—what did that mean? . . . Was it really possible that he had killed his brother?"[3]

The story means that man's unity was disintegrated; his oneness in a family under God was fragmented.

> Then the LORD said to Cain, "Where is Abel your brother?" He said, "I do not know; am I my brother's keeper?" And the LORD said, "What have you done? The voice of your brother's blood is crying to me from the ground."[4]

Thus was begun the long road to exile and estrangement that winds yet through the labyrinthian ways of the human heart.

It is the story of us all, caught as we are in the net of good and evil. Abel dies. He fades into the shadows. Only Cain survives. For a time, at least, only Cain had children. It was only through Cain that the human race was perpetuated. True, there

is another tradition in the book of Genesis of a third son of
Adam and Eve—one named Seth—born after Abel was killed,
through whom the lineage is traced. The descendants of Cain are
listed without comment, but are we not all in some sense descendants of Cain? We try to disregard our similarity. But it is
not that easy. *All* people are begotten of Cain. It is not so easy
to hide our kinship.

For his story is reenacted whenever a man's blood shed by his
brother cries out to God from the ground. It is the story of Vietnam, of giant bombers over Hanoi and Haiphong, of hand-to-
hand combat in places like Hue and An Loc. It is the story of
a man in the kitchen of a Los Angeles hotel with a handgun and
murder in his heart. It is the story of another man in a darkened
motel in Memphis with a rifle placed to his shoulder. It is the
story of still another man with a pistol in a crowded shopping
center in Laurel, Maryland.

We are shocked, dismayed, grieved. For we know, deep in-
side, that it is in some sense the story of us all. We are all children of Cain, murderer of his brother. We are children of Cain,
not Abel, who died without issue. We resist the knowledge of
our heritage. We reject our ancestry. We try not to remember
the details, but the dark record is there.

> Cain knew his wife, and she conceived and bore Enoch;
> and he built a city, and called the name of the city after the
> name of his son, Enoch.[5]

Who is Cain? He is the stranger, the alienated one. "Am I
my brother's keeper?" he cries out defiantly to God. Thus he de-
clares his separateness, his irresponsibility. Albert Camus' novel
The Stranger begins thus:

> Mother died today. Or, maybe, yesterday; I can't be sure.
> The telegram from the Home says: YOUR MOTHER PASSED
> AWAY. FUNERAL TOMORROW. DEEP SYMPATHY. Which leaves the
> matter doubtful; it could have been yesterday.[6]

This is Camus' way of underlining the Stranger's detachment
from affection and human relationships. To him, life and death
are all the same in a world that he has abandoned, in a world

in which neither love nor individuals to love even exist. He is the stranger who, "at certain moments, confronts us in a mirror,"[7] the stranger within who no longer cares, who leads us to abandon our brotherhood, to remain uninvolved. He is the one who asks, "Am I my brother's keeper?" and then remains silent, as that first Cain did.

Thus we are members of Cain's family. He is our father, and we are his children who look upon our brothers and ask, "Am I my brother's keeper?" The history of man is determined by the Cain spirit.

Who is Cain? He is the estranged one, the wanderer.

> Then Cain went away from the presence of the LORD, and dwelt in the land of Nod, east of Eden.[8]

"Nod" means "wandering." It is a valid symbol, for Cain dwelt in the land of wandering. The land of wandering became his home forever. It is still home for the sons of Cain, still home for all of us, this land of Nod, of wandering. Jacques Ellul makes this point: "We will leave to the historians such remarks as, 'Geographers know of no land of Nod.' When I first read it, that sentence set me to dreaming. Unknown, to geographers! And what kind of land would it be, this Nowhere land, which is not a place but a lack of place, the opposite of Eden, another country unknown to geographers?"[9] Eden, Nod,—unknown to geographers but known to our hearts.

What kind of land is the land of Nod? The kind we find ourselves in where love is unknown and brotherhood is denied. Do you ever feel that you are dwelling in the land of wandering —apart from the world, apart from God himself? Did you ever feel bereft and alone? Ever want to timidly reach out a hand and touch someone just to reassure yourself? And then, do you ever look with compassion upon life and wish that you could bring Cain and Abel together again?

As the young Russian poet Yevtushenko, when he was in this country, explained: "I write poems about Vietnam and Babi Yar and Kent University student Allison Krause and a Siberian concrete-pourer, Nyushka, and a general in the army of freedom,

Pancho Villa, and my own mother, who lost her voice singing concerts in snowstorms on the front lines, and a Chilean prostitute who hung a portrait of Leo Tolstoy in her closet, and Sicilian women in black and young girls in white and my own beloved and my son and myself. I want to be a mail boat for everyone divided by the ice of estrangement . . . moving through the drifting ice with letters and parcels." [10]

This image of a mail boat is a magnificent figure in a world of Cains and Abels. A packet sailing to the land of Nod with a message for the Cain in all men: "Come back! Come back to Eden where your brother is." We are all wanderers at times. "Where is God?" we ask. And then, like Cain, we feel, "My punishment is greater than I can bear."

Did Cain feel that he was too wicked to know the mercy of God? Men and women guilty of less heinous crimes than murder have so felt. Of the nineteenth-century Danish philosopher Soren Kierkegaard, it has been said by one of his interpreters: "Throughout his whole life the great difficulty was to arrive at a personal sense of having been forgiven. . . . To believe that God actually had forgotten his sins required, according to Kierkegaard, so great a courage that it would hardly be realized in the experience of more than ten persons in each generation." [11] That is what the Cain in us, the wanderer in us, the estranged one in us, keeps telling us. So we cherish our guilt. We fondle it. We remain unforgiven.

Guilt is real. But there are different kinds of guilt. There is a genuine guilt that is healthy. It means our acknowledgment of our need of the forgiveness of God and our brothers. There is the neurotic guilt that is unhealthy and destructive. Edward Stein says: "What genuine guilt (remorse) cares about is that *a personal relationship has been broken, love has been wronged.* The sadness that ensues is normal and natural, as when a friend has gone or been injured. What *neurotic* guilt cares about is that the self may be punished or love must be recovered. It is narcissistic and concerned about this punishment more than reconciliation with the other." [12]

Cain concentrated on his punishment ("My punishment is

greater than I can bear"), not on his broken relationship with his dead brother, his parents, his God. He cries:

> "Behold, thou hast driven me this day away from the ground; and from thy face I shall be hidden; and I shall be a fugitive and a wanderer on the earth, and whoever finds me will slay me." [13]

There is an amazing arrogance in us, at times, that makes us think our sins are too big for the grace of God. This really amounts to the presumption that we are such evildoers that God must turn from us because we are too much for him. So, we dwell in the land of Nod, unforgiven. We are footsore and travel stained, going our painful ways of self-laceration. We cannot love because we do not feel we are loved. We cannot accept our brothers because we feel unacceptable to the Father. Like Cain, we are fugitives and wanderers from the relaitonships that heal and mend.

But God is still like God. The writer says that "the LORD put a mark on Cain, lest any who came upon him should kill him." [14]

The mark of Cain is badly misinterpreted. The mark of Cain was the sign of God that he was the watched-over man, watched over by God. The mark of Cain was the mark of God's concern for him. It was the gentle sign of God's continuing concern for Cain the murderer, the slayer of his brother. The ancient writer came to the daring, illogical conclusion that no one can stray so far that he is beyond the reached-out hand of God. If Cain remained impenitent, unforgiven, it was Cain's choice, not God's. Some unknown poet added to this primitive account of brokenness and betrayal of love the hint of what Ernest Campbell calls "God's pursuing, non-stop shatter-proof love for the world." [15] This love is finally expressed on a cross in the figure who cried out, "Father, forgive them; for they know not what they do." This takes your breath away, if you think a minute, and then it lets you breathe again.

There it is for whatever it is worth to you, the mark of Cain upon each of us, at last. Not the murderer's mark but the mark of watched-over-by-God Cain. Breathe out, in gratitude, in acceptance, you watched-over ones.

The Adventure of Hope

Once upon a time there was a man named Abraham. The name means "father of a multitude." To him are traced the origins of the Jewish people, and they are still called "Sons of Abraham." He is important as an individual and important as a symbol. His name is found in twenty-seven of the sixty-six books of the Bible, found there more than three hundred times.

As a symbol, he represents the long-ago migration of certain nomadic tribes who became the people of Israel, migrating from Ur of the Chaldees westward toward Palestine. As a symbol, he is more than an individual; he is a migration of clans. More, as a symbol, he represents the outward thrust of the human spirit, the adventuring movement of a daring impulse, responding to an inner vision. Centuries after Abraham, the author of the Letter to the Hebrews defines faith as "the assurance of things hoped for, the conviction of things not seen." Then, he proceeds to illustrate the functioning of faith in the lives of heroes of old. He sets down the names of Abel and Enoch and Noah. And then he puts down the name of Abraham and waxes lyrical:

> By faith Abraham obeyed when, he was called to go out to a place which he was to receive as an inheritance; and he went out, not knowing where he was to go. By faith he sojourned in the land of promise, as in a foreign land, living in tents with Isaac and Jacob, heirs with him of the same promise. For he looked forward to the city which has foundations, whose builder and maker is God.[1]

Paul uses this man, in the Letter to the Romans, as the supreme example of what he means by justification of faith, a living out of faith. Then, in the Letter to the Galatians, he uses him as the supreme example of one who believed the promises of God and acted upon them. Matthew traces the genealogy of Jesus back to Abraham and sees no need to go any further to

25

establish Jesus' credentials. The rabbis had a tradition that Abraham would welcome the faithful into Paradise. In fact, the phrase "Abraham's bosom" became synonymous with Paradise in Jewish tradition. Jesus reflects it in the sixteenth chapter of the Gospel according to Luke, when he tells this story:

> There was a rich man, who was clothed in purple and fine linen and who feasted sumptuously every day. And at his gate lay a poor man named Lazarus, full of sores, who desired to be fed with what fell from the rich man's table; moreover the dogs came and licked his sores. The poor man died and was carried by the angels to Abraham's bosom. The rich man also died and was buried; and in Hades, being in torment, he lifted up his eyes, and saw Abraham far off and Lazarus in his bosom. And he called out, "Father Abraham, have mercy upon me, and send Lazarus to dip the end of his finger in water and cool my tongue; for I am in anguish in this flame." [2]

Once upon a time there was a man named Abraham. There came a burning in his breast, a trembling in his limbs, a turning and twisting in the night. And he arose and struck his tents and left for a land of promise.

Once upon a time there was a man named Abraham. There came a voice calling, a hand beckoning, a finger pointing. And he set out for tomorrow not knowing where he was going.

Once upon a time there was a man named Abraham. What do we really know about him as an individual? Not much. A series of vignettes in the book of Genesis, not all of them appealing. In fact, some of them are rather appalling, like that shabby little incident when he went down to Egypt because of famine.

> When he was about to enter Egypt, he said to Sarai his wife, "I know that you are a woman beautiful to behold; and when the Egyptians see you, they will say, 'This is his wife'; then they will kill me, but they will let you live. Say you are my sister, that it may go well with me because of you, and that my life may be spared on your account." [3]

And, sure enough, Pharaoh's courtiers saw her, saw that she was beautiful, and she was taken to Pharaoh's harem. Pharaoh emerges from this episode looking bigger than Abraham, for when he found out what had happened, he called Abraham and said.

"What is this you have done to me? Why did you not tell me that she was your wife? Why did you say, 'She is my sister,' so that I took her for my wife? Now then, here is your wife, take her, and be gone." [4]

Of course, we must remember this was a different stage of human history. Women were chattels and polygamy was standard practice. In spite of that episode, the relationship between Abraham and Sarah came to be a tender and enduring one. They spent a long life together. And at the end of it, so the story goes: "Sarah lived a hundred and twenty-seven years; these were the years of the life of Sarah. And Sarah died at Kiriatharba (that is, Hebron) in the land of Canaan; and Abraham went in to mourn for Sarah and to weep for her." [5]

He was a man of generous impulses, or so it would seem at times, at least. Lot, his nephew, was a shyster. He and Uncle Abraham got along pretty well together, but their herdsmen and their servants clashed. Abraham suggested that they separate in order to keep the peace. He asked Lot:

> "Is not the whole land before you? Separate yourself from me. If you take the left hand, then I will go to the right; or if you take the right hand, then I will go to the left." And Lot lifted up his eyes, and saw that the Jordan valley was well watered everywhere like the garden of the LORD, like the land of Egypt, in the direction of Zoar . . . . Abraham dwelt in the land of Canaan, while Lot . . . . moved his tent as far as Sodom.[6]

There is no evidence that Abraham even protested at this greedy choice on Lot's part of the best land. He was apparently a man of generous impulses. There was the time when he interceded with God for the city of Sodom, marked for destruction.

> Then the LORD said, "Because the outcry against Sodom and Gomorrah is great and their sin is very grave, I will go down to see whether they have done altogether according to the outcry which has come to me. . . ."
> . . . Then Abraham drew near, and said, "Wilt thou indeed destroy the righteous with the wicked? Suppose there are fifty righteous within the city; wilt thou then destroy the place and not spare it for the fifty righteous who are in it? Far be it from thee to do such a thing, to slay the righteous with the

wicked, so that the righteous fare as the wicked! Far be that from thee! Shall not the Judge of all the earth do right? And the LORD said, "If I find at Sodom fifty righteous in the city, I will spare the whole place for their sake." [7]

And so Abraham tried to work him down gradually. Forty-five. Forty. Thirty. Twenty. Ten. Evidently, he did not get low enough. The story goes that Sodom was destroyed. Abraham had his streaks of tenderness and compassion, traits which were not commonly noted in desert shieks.

But none of these things are the things for which he comes front and center so often in the Biblical narrative and the Hebrew tradition. The thing for which he stands to the fore is his faith— that tremendous faith that kept him and led him through disappointment and beyond failure. It was more than a stubborn, teeth-clenched kind of faith. It was marked by imagination and by openness to new insights.

Abraham is almost as prominent in Mohammedan legend and tradition as he is in Jewish. The Persian poet Saadi records a tale that illustrates Abraham's openness:

> One day when Abraham sat at his tent-door, according to his custom, waiting to entertain strangers, he espied an old man stooping and leaning on his staffe, weary with age and travelle, coming toward him, who was an hundred years of age; [Abraham] received him kindly, washed his feet, provided supper, caused him to sit down; but observing that the old man ate and prayed not, nor begged for a blessing on his meat, asked him why he did not worship the God of heaven. The old man told him that he worshipped the fire only, and acknowledged no other God: at which answer Abraham grew so zealously angry, that he thrust the old man out of his tent, and exposed him to all the evils of the night and an unguarded condition. When the old man was gone, [God] called to him and asked him where the stranger was; he replied, 'I thrust him away because he did not worship thee'; [God] answered him, 'I have suffered him these hundred years, although he dishonored me, and couldst thou not endure him one night, when he gave thee no trouble?' Upon this, saith the story, Abraham fetch him back again, and gave him hospitable entertainment and wise instruction.[8]

Perhaps the most often repeated illustration of the faith of

Abraham is that story of the sacrifice of his son, Isaac. He took the son of his and Sarah's old age to a hilltop altar in the full belief that the voice of God was telling him to sacrifice his son. Then, even as he was about to plunge the knife into the boy's breast, another voice told him not to consummate the deed. I remember how, as a lad in Sunday school, this bothered me, especially that point that was so often made, that unctuous point, that because Abraham was willing to do such a thing, he proved his faith and let himself off the hook. Somehow that never rang true, for it did not let God off the hook for me.

Years later, the point came to me that this story centers in Abraham's rejection of what was a perfectly orthodox view of God. Child sacrifice was a common feature of Canaanite ritual. Abraham, as a product of that crude society, accepted it as a normal expression, a way of propitiating the gods. His daring rejection of such a barbaric rite marked an outward bound of the human spirit, a long stride away from the concept of a dark deity who commands such violation of normal emotions. Abraham's faith was a faith willing to break through things, willing to break out of past customs and traditional practices. The impact comes at his hearing and obeying another inner voice saying, "Do not lay your hand on the lad." That was the point, the revolutionary point, a revolutionary advance in the concept of the relationship between God and man, man and God.

To break with the past is sometimes necessary. Faith always carries within it an element of risk, else it is not faith. It involves, at times, the abandonment of the security of thought and custom and place. For men of Abraham's time, the gods were placated by human sacrifice. When Abraham moved away from such an idea and beyond such a custom, he had to move by faith as surely as when he left Ur of the Chaldees for that Promised Land.

And us? Is life lost—while we plod around in circles? Something lost—because we have not moved spiritually beyond our mother's knee? Or out of the kindergarten intellectually?

Faith is a venture through confidence in God's grace. Faith is always on the move. We know what it is to be literally on the move. We are the most mobile people in modern history. Two out of five families will move within the next twelve months. My great, great grandfather, many generations back, settled in North Carolina before the American Revolution. For 150 years his son's sons lived in the same town, usually in the same house. In a little over one-third of that period of time, I have lived in eight different states, eleven cities and towns. I am not untypical of my generation. I think we know what it is to move emotionally and intellectually. All of us have found that in order to live in our world we have had to abandon old positions, sometimes reluctantly, sometimes gladly. There are enduring values that we dare not abandon. There are positions that we cannot leave and make sense out of life. But each of us, finally, must find for himself the values that endure, and stake out positions for himself. However, the biggest question—the framework within which all of this decision-making is set—is the question, Do we go with God, or do we just go?

The man named Abraham decided he would go with God, as he understood him, and he went seeking a city, following the promises of God—a sojourner by faith, a traveler in hope, an adventurer by grace. For faith is a venture, but it is not a blind venture. It is a venture in hope. In his *Critique of Pure Reason,* Immanuel Kant wrote: "The whole interest of reason, speculative as well as practical, is centered in the three following questions: (1) What can I know? (2) What ought I to do? (3) What may I hope?" [9]

Our age is concentrated on "What can I know?" The religious emphasis in our time has seemed to be upon "What ought I to do?" Important as these questions are, they fade before the third for an age in transition such as ours: "What may I hope?" What may I hope in a world that is torn by war? What can I hope in a world where there are uncertainties politically, socially, economically? What can I hope in a world of division? What can I hope for my life? The question "What may I hope?" involves the whole thrust and direction of my being. What is hope and faith on the move? Faith, keeping stride with courage, headed somewhere.

Abraham lived on hope through the promises of God, an adventurer moving toward a city, "not knowing where he was going." But who does? Who knows where a marriage is going when it is consummated? Who knows where a career is going when it is entered upon? Who knows what a child is going to be when he is born? Who knows what will happen? We have to live by faith and by hope. We have to, to take one step toward the future. The question is, faith in whom and hope for what?

A little paper, issued by the Department on the Laity of the World Council of Churches a few years ago, entitled "Man in One and Many Worlds" begins like this:

> Stop that roadmaking gang! People cause one another harm without being brought closer. Stop that surgeon! That man whom he is rescuing from death will be back to exploit his fellow-men. Stop that scientist, who is on the verge of producing life! What monsters may be born if his discoveries fall into unscrupulous hands? Stop that woman from giving birth! Who can tell whether her child will be a Hitler or a Marie Curie?
>
> Men go on making roads. Surgeons heal without enquiring into the morals or worth of their patients. Scientists take the risk of letting the knowledge and power they gain pass into other human hands. Women bear children with no guarantee beforehand regarding their sex, their future health, or their future character.[10]

Do we not commit these acts of faith in the future, these daily ordinary acts, because we cannot do otherwise and be human? Are we not destined to adventure into grace by faith? Are we not predestined to hope by our very nature? Are we not creatures of hope, all in some way seekers of a city "whose builder and maker is God"? So, we go on through our little lives, discouraged at times, wondering sometimes in the night, and then waking with the daylight still going on.

Once upon a time there was a man named Abraham. "By faith Abraham obeyed when he was called to go out to a place which he was to receive as an inheritance." [11] And he went, not knowing where he was going.

Past the Breaking Places

Once upon a time there was a city named Sodom. It was a very wicked city, so the story goes. Its name has been immortalized in indelicate fashion. It was one of the five cities of the plain of the Jordan River. Exactly where it was located we can no longer tell, for it was destroyed many, many centuries ago. Geological and archaeological evidence would indicate that Sodom and the other cities of the plain were located in an area now submerged under the waters of the southern part of the Dead Sea. Its ruin was probably caused by a great earthquake, accompanied by explosions, lightning, ignition of natural gases, and general conflagration.

Sodom was a city so sated with evil, so saturated in vice and perversity, that its destruction was attributed by the ancient storyteller to the judgment of a God who could no longer stomach it, a city so wicked that even today Sodom and her sister city, Gomorrah, are proverbial expression of urban degeneracy and human decay. In the dictionary, "Sodom" is now defined as "a city or country notorious for vice and corruption." But our story is not about a city except as a setting for a human tragedy, a very personal tragedy, even a small human tragedy in the light of the destruction of five cities.

Once upon a time there was a woman, the wife of a man named Lot, and so the story goes. Let me recapitulate it from Genesis 19:

> The two angels came to Sodom in the evening; and Lot was sitting in the gate of Sodom. When Lot saw them, he rose to meet them, and bowed himself with his face to the earth, and said, "My lords, turn aside, I pray you, to your servant's house and spend the night, and wash your feet; then you may rise up early and go on your way." . . .
> Then the men said to Lot, "Have you any one else here?

> Sons-in-law, sons, daughters, or any one you have in the city,
> bring them out of the place; for we are about to destroy this
> place, because the outcry against its people has become great
> before the LORD, and the LORD has sent us to destroy it.". . .
> When morning dawned, the angels urged Lot, saying, "Arise,
> take your wife and your two daughters who are here, lest you
> be consumed in the punishment of the city. . . . Flee for your
> life; do not look back or stop anywhere in the valley; flee to
> the hills, lest you be consumed.". . .
> Then the LORD rained on Sodom and Gomorrah brimstone
> and fire from the LORD out of heaven; and he overthrew those
> cities, and all the valley, and all the inhabitants of the cities,
> and what grew on the ground. But Lot's wife behind him looked
> back, and she became a pillar of salt.[1]

"Press on," said the angel. "Do not look back." But back
there were all the things that she had loved. That tumbling, blaz-
ing city was the place of her home with its familiar furnishings,
the streets through which she had walked proud and haughty,
the wife of a successful man. Back there were her memories.
Back there were her roots. Ahead of her? A long, long road
stretching into the dark. At the end of it, a little town and a
terrible emptiness, the pain of starting life all over in middle
years. Back there the known, ahead the unknown. Back there!
And she stopped. Her husband and children, intent on their own
escape, did not notice. "Go on," the angel had said. "Don't
look back." How could she help it? How could she keep from
pausing, for a moment at least, to relive the past? "Go on, go
on," said the voice. What could even an angel know of a woman's heart? She stopped, she turned, she looked back, and whatever happened, happened. Was it the explosion of a nearby bi-
tuminous well? A volcanic eruption which flung up the waters of
the salty sea over her and caught her as she stood? Whatever
happened, happened. To the storyteller, it was simple. "Lot's
wife behind him looked back, and she became a pillar of salt."

First, some kind words for Lot's wife. Her act was understandable. She did a very human thing. Kurt Vonnegut, in an
introduction to his novel *Slaughterhouse-Five,* tells of his ad-
miration for Lot's wife, who in spite of the divine command
looked back at a city crashing and crumbling, where moments

before, people (admittedly vile, but human beings) lived. "But she *did* look back," says Vonnegut, "and I love her for that, because it was so human." [2] Why? What for? What did she expect to see? Dorothy Leiser puts her thoughts into a little verse:

> It wasn't the fire
> or falling stone
> I turned back to see.
> It was a vision
> of children playing on the roof;
> the morning sun on a muddy street . . .
> the way it used to be. [3]

Yes, the way it used to be. The trouble sometimes, in seeking the vision of the way it used to be, is that we can be halted in our tracks, we can be frozen into immobility. "Go on," said the voice. You may call it the voice of an angel or just the inexorability of life. But it is there. For life is always in motion, always in process of becoming something else. It is never static. Oh, not motion for motion's sake, not a churning about for the sake of churning. I do not mean that kind of nervous activity and impulsive leaping that sometimes characterizes us. I do not mean the strenuous life that leads to emotional exhaustion and a nervous breakdown. I mean the process of motion, the life process unrelated to physical activity or even mental energy. It is a growth process. It is the acceptance of each moment that we live as comprising the fullness of time.

Eugen Rosenstock-Huessy has written that man's life is always at "a crossroads between four 'fronts': backward toward the past; forward toward the future; inward among ourselves, our feelings, our wishes, our dreams; and outward against what we must fight or exploit or come to terms with or ignore." [4] We must be constantly making decisions on four fronts, deciding what to leave behind, what to reach for, what to come to terms with within, what to relate to without. Life is perpetual decision, sometimes not even conscious decision. Sometimes circumstances make decisions for us.

Childhood is the time for leaving infancy behind. Adolescence is the time for leaving childhood behind. The adolescent has to forfeit the securities of childhood in order to assume the increased responsibility and the freedom of growing up. Manhood and womanhood constitute a time for leaving adolescence behind. There is a mingled sadness and joy at all of these breaking points in life, but they must be accomplished.

Cartoonist Hank Ketcham years ago came home to a wife suffering the exasperation of a long day with a small boy. "Hank," she said, "our son Dennis is a menace." [5] That started it. Ketcham knew a good idea when he heard one. So year after year, Dennis goes on being an uninhibited menace in Ketcham's cartoons, and we laugh at him. He does what he pleases, says what he wants, takes what he needs if he can get it. But the cartoonist keeps him always a small boy, never lets him grow up. For if he lets Dennis grow up into a gangling adolescent still tormenting Mr. Wilson and insulting Margaret, it would no longer be funny. He would be just another juvenile delinquent. To grow up, Dennis must leave his uninhibited self-centeredness behind. To grow up is a little sad.

John Updike says of one of his characters in *Rabbit Redux:* "It comes to him: growth is betrayal. There is no other route. There is no arriving somewhere without leaving somewhere." [6] We are always moving from somewhere to somewhere, as Lot and his family were moving from Sodom to the little mountain town of Zoar. T. S. Eliot says in *Four Quartets:*

> Home is where one starts from. As we grow older
> The world becomes stranger, the pattern more complicated
> Of dead and living. Not the intense moment
> Isolated, with no before and after,
> But a lifetime burning in every moment
> And not the lifetime of one man only
> But of old stones that cannot be deciphered. [7]

And there is an element of urgency about it all that hangs over so many of our departures. There are certain times of leaving when there is no sense of insistence, of intensity, or of pressure. The mother at the door, watching a child go off to school for the first time, has an intermingled sense of sadness and pride and relief. But other departures carry with them an intensity of feeling and the harsh realization that life will never be the same again. Death is one, the most complete one. There are places of breaking. There is in life, over and over again, the sound of a door closing. "Go on," says life. "You can't go back." We know, no matter how desperately we want to, we cannot go back to some things. We know how important it is to keep on going on. We know but . . . it is hard at times.

The point of Jesus' use of the story of Lot's wife was the need to react decisively at the time of a catastrophic event. Jesus said, "On that day, let him who is on the housetop, with his goods in the house, not come down to take them away; and likewise let him who is in the field not turn back. Remember Lot's wife." [8]

God's grace goes with us past the breaking places. God may have been with us in Sodom. But will he not be with us in Zoar, too? He is ahead of us, always, out there. He is with us in the changes, the transitions of life, amid our lost securities. He is with us in a very gentle way. That is the point. We move into grace out of our graceless and awkward clinging to that which is over in life.

Once upon a time there was a woman. We do not know her name. Jewish tradition calls her Edith. But to the Biblical story-teller she was just "Lot's wife," who became a symbol, a warning symbol. The historian Josephus wrote in the first century in his *Antiquities of the Jews* that a pillar of salt still existed.[9] W. H. Bennett, modern commentator on the Bible, wrote: "Recently, at any rate, there was still standing, on the hill of Usdum, at the southwest end of the Dead Sea, 'a high round pillar of crystalline salt about forty feet high.' This may be the pillar referred to by Josephus . . . and perhaps that which tradition had in view from the outset." [10]

At any rate, she was immortalized, this woman who looked back. Poor Edith, if that was her name. "Go on, go with God." She just could not.

Story of a Stranger in the Night

Once upon a time there was a man named Jacob. His saga is filled with strange and wondrous tales. But of them all the story of his wrestling with the stranger at the ford of the Jobbak River is the strangest. In fact, it is one of the strangest tales in all of the Old Testament.

Jacob is returning from his long exile in the north Arabian desert, an exile forced upon him by the wrath of his brother, Esau, whom he had cheated of his birthright. He is nervously nearing home and his first encounter with the brother whom he had defrauded. The night before the confrontation, he sends his wives, his children, and his servants across the river. He remains on the opposite bank alone.

"And Jacob was left alone; and a man wrestled with him until the breaking of the day. When the man saw that he did not prevail against Jacob, he touched the hollow of his thigh; and Jacob's thigh was put out of joint as he wrestled with him. Then he said, 'Let me go, for the day is breaking.' But Jacob said, 'I will not let you go, unless you bless me.' And he said to him, 'What is your name?' And he said, 'Jacob.' Then he said, 'Your name shall no more be called Jacob, but Israel, for you have striven with God and with men, and have prevailed.' Then Jacob asked him, 'Tell me, I pray, your name.' But he said, 'Why is it that you ask my name?' And there he blessed him. So Jacob called the name of the place Peniel, saying, 'For I have seen God face to face, and yet my life is preserved.' The sun rose upon him as he passed Penuel, limping because of his thigh." [1] A strange and fascinating story! What do you make of it?

Who was that stranger in the night? According to primitive myth, a river god guarded every stream to resist those who attempted to pass over. Was this the origin of the story? "A man wrestled with Jacob," says the chronicler. And yet, when the tale is done, Jacob says, "I have seen God face to face." Surely, this is a strange God who comes hurling himself out of the darkness, contending in physical combat with a man; a God who, when dawn comes, cries, "Let me go, for the day is breaking," and to whom the man replies, "I will not let you go, unless you bless me." One interpreter of this passage asks: "A ghost, a demon? . . . It is an ancient, jagged-edged story, dangerous and crude as a stone knife. If it means anything, what does it mean, and let us not assume that it means anything very neat or very edifying." [2] It can mean little to the plodding, literalist mind, yet it may mean much to the poet.

For if it means anything, it means something primitive, something very elemental about human experience. Hand to hand, belly to belly, eyeball to eyeball—there is a struggle here for an understanding of the self by Jacob. Let us not forget the history of this man. His was a sorry story of self-seeking and self-aggrandizement. His life had been graceless and crude, twisted by treachery. First he had cheated his brother, Esau, out of his birthright. Then he had defrauded Esau of their father's blessing. Among the ancients, the father's blessing was not simply kind words and a pat on the head or even a financial patrimony. It was deeply rooted in religious connotations. A father's blessing was believed to contain power. There was a divine dimension to the father's blessing. Once spoken, it could not be reclaimed, it could not be recalled. In Jacob's case, the blessing of the father, Isaac, belonged to Esau, the oldest son. Yet Jacob deceived his blind father shamelessly and received the blessing for himself.

Such chicanery was in keeping with the entire career of this man. He carried on his deceitful encounters with his father-in-law, Laban, over the years. Laban was a man whose shabbiness could match that of Jacob's own. In short, Jacob was a schemer, a liar, a coward, among other things. He was an opportunist and a sly deceiver. "What is your name?" the dark antagonist asked. In ancient times, a man's name was far more than a handle to go by. The name was intimately related to the nature of the man. It was thus of far more substance than a mere mark of identification, for to ask a man's name in ancient times was, in a very deep sense, to ask "Who are you?" "Jacob" was the reply, and the name told who the man was. For "Jacob" means "he who supplants; he who takes someone else's place by trickery or treachery." This was Jacob, the Supplanter. Against the night he flung the name. Against the night he confessed who he was, Jacob, the unworthy deceiver.

There are other strange twists to this story. For one, there is the fact that through the hours of the struggle, according to the chronicler, the man saw that he did not prevail against Jacob. As the daybreak came, he asked, "Let me go, for the day is breaking." Jacob was winning the contest. Then the stranger touches the hollow of his thigh, and in a moment, it is all reversed. Jacob lies crippled, defeated. According to ancient legend, says W. Robertson Smith, the hollow of the thigh was sacred as the seat of life.[3] As you read the story of this struggle in the night, you have the feeling that it was all inevitable and fated, the feeling that Jacob was engaged in a contest he could not win, that even his temporary superiority, when he seemed to prevail, was destined to be overwhelmed. Only in defeat does the final confrontation come. "I will not let you go, unless you bless me," says Jacob, clinging desperately to his antagonist. "What is your name?"—and the blessing comes in defeat. "Your name shall no more be called Jacob, but Israel," which means "he who strives with God." While Jacob lay crippled and broken, hanging on desperately, he gained a new name, symbolic of a new personality. No longer was he Jacob, the Supplanter, but Israel, the Wrestler with God.

We have theologies of triumph. We have no theology of defeat. We have theologies for those who are victorious over adversity, those who smile through their tears, who keep their chins up no matter what comes. But what of the defeated person who, pride broken, arrogance dispelled, lies helpless on his back; the person who cannot rise; the person who has been crippled at the core of his being, who has been touched in the hollow of his thigh. Walt Whitman sings:

> Have you heard that it was good to gain the day?
> I also say it is good to fall—
>   battles are lost in the same spirit
>   in which they are won.[4]

Jacob's blessing came at the instant of his crushing.

There are two other strange aspects of this long-ago story to which I wish to point your attention. One is Jacob's request: "Tell me, I pray, your name." And the answer: "Why is it that you ask my name?" Here was an answer that was no answer at all. It was another question, and the mystery of who that stranger was remained. Was he man, ghost, demon, angel? Jacob never knew, but he did know, through the mystery of anonymity, that there was meaning. "Jacob called the name of the place Peniel, saying, 'For I have seen God face to face . . .' "

Finally, it must be recognized that Jacob continued to bear the marks of his encounter. "The sun rose upon him as he passed Penuel, limping because of his thigh." Some defeats are victories. Out of some defeats blessings come when men see God face to face. Both defeat and blessing left their marks forever. The glaring dawn comes. Jacob limps into the future, changed and marked and stamped indelibly.

You can never tell when this will happen, the defeat and the blessing together. For Jacob it happened as he returned triumphantly home, successful, rich. It happened as he returned to the place from which he had fled ignominiously into the wilderness but a few short years before. Now he was back to show the home folks what he had done in life, but the homecoming proved to be more than he had expected. Waiting for the climactic moment of that homecoming, he underwent his shattering experience. It was a time of reckoning as times of reckoning come for most of us.

Some of us get by without any time of reckoning. We live our lives out, carefully measuring love and involvement by the teaspoonful. We avoid any real confrontation with ourselves or with others. We push aside all experiences that raise questions, that cause unease within our spirits. We wonder at times, perhaps, who we are or what we are. Then we shake off the wonder and ignore the questions that come. We refuse to probe beneath the surface of our experiences. There is so much upon the surface to keep us occupied—the world events that threaten to engulf us, the domestic concerns that encompass us, the private problems that tease us and haunt us. There is enough to attend to without probing into the meaning of life.

Then some midnight hour strikes. A ghost? A demon? A man? An angel? Whoever he may be, a stranger comes in the night and you are a wrestler, grappling fiercely in hand-to-hand, eyeball-to-eyeball contact. Old anxieties walk softly in the night, old insecurities tug at your spirit, old treasons leer from the shadows in the corners, and old memories dance upon the ceiling. And you hang on grimly, desperately, waiting for the day. You must receive a blessing! You must move from graceless to grace-filled living! You must find new hope, fresh determination! You cannot face the new day without it. You must know what you are. You must know your name. You are Jacob, the Supplanter. You must know who you can be. Jacob, defeated, touched in the hollow of his thigh, became Israel who prevailed with God. Who can you become? Who can I?

Harry Emerson Fosdick, whose preaching always manifested a buoyant faith, once told his congregation how in his young manhood he had gone through an emotional breakdown. In a sermon preached toward the end of his long service at Riverside Church in New York, he said: "It was the most terrifying wilderness I ever traveled through. . . . My little book, *The Meaning of Prayer,* would never have been written without that breakdown. I found God in a desert."[5]

Ultimately, you look back, and realization comes that unbeknown you wrestled once in the night with God. The realization may not come until it is all over. That was Jacob's experience. When the day came finally, the sun hot and high, he said with awe, "I have seen God face to face."

And us? Perhaps we have seen him and not known it. Some sorrow before which we have stared hot-eyed into the night. Some loss that came, and our pain, laced with resentment, left us unable to pray. Some wrong done to someone, and the awful, overwhelming feeling came that our treachery was so great that we could never forgive ourselves. Some wrong done to us, and there was that hard lump of hate in the breast that would not melt and allow us to forgive another. Some temptation that we felt we could not hold out against yet knew that we must, for to yield to it would be to destroy ourselves. In the knowledge of any of these things, we have wrestled in the night with God.

And with the dawn, exhausted, we must go back to life again, but limping, shamed, changed, stunned, at the feelings of which we suddenly discover ourselves capable. What did we see when the light broke? What did Jacob see? Is that the last glimpse we have of him—limping toward home, awkward, twisted, graceless?

No, that is not the last glimpse we have of Jacob. We see him the next day, standing twisted and deformed on his ruined hip. And his brother, Esau, says the chronicler, "ran to meet him, and fell on his neck and kissed him, and they wept." [6] Jacob had come home to his brother, to God. Purged, forgiven, renewed, he had come home.

Holding Things Together

Once upon a time there was a man named Isaac. The name means "son of laughter" or "laughing one." The name came from the circumstances surrounding the birth of Isaac. Once, as his father, Abraham, sat at the door of his tent in the heat of the day, three mysterious strangers came along. Abraham hospitably afforded them water for their feet and food for their bellies. After they had eaten, according to the storyteller: "They said to him, 'Where is Sarah your wife?' And he said, 'She is in the tent.' The LORD said, 'I will surely return to you in the spring, and Sarah your wife shall have a son.' And Sarah was listening at the tent door behind him. Now Abraham and Sarah were old, advanced in age; it had ceased to be with Sarah after the manner of women. So Sarah laughed to herself, saying, 'After I have grown old, and my husband is old, shall I have pleasure?' The LORD said to Abraham, 'Why did Sarah laugh, and say, "Shall I indeed bear a child, now that I am old?" Is anything too hard for the LORD? At the appointed time I will return to you, in the spring, and Sarah shall have a son.' But Sarah denied, saying, 'I did not laugh'; for she was afraid. He said, 'No, but you did laugh.' " [1] She laughed, all right. It was a laughing matter.

Nevertheless, centuries later, when the author of the Letter to the Hebrews calls the roll of the faithful, he includes Sarah in the list. She is the first woman in the list. Furthermore, she is the only cynic. She laughed at a word from God. She laughed, all right. It was a laughing matter, when you think about her situation. But when the time came, a son was born, and she named him Isaac—the son of laughter, the laughing one.

So Isaac was the son of a hardheaded, clear-eyed daughter of fact who could not easily believe that at age ninety she would conceive and bear a son. Still, she believed God faithful and

45

remembered the promise even in her skepticism. So, when the child was born she said, "God has given me good reason to laugh, and everybody who hears will laugh with me."[2] Isaac was the son of realistic Sarah and idealistic Abraham. Abraham, his father, had set out years before from Ur of the Chaldees in search of a city "which has foundations, whose builder and maker is God." He had left his ancestral home without knowing where he was going. He was a follower of a promise, a pursuer of a dream. There had come a burning in his breast, a trembling in his limbs, a turning and twisting in the night. And he rose, struck his tents, and left his homeland for a land of promise. Such was Abraham, Isaac's father. Both he and Sarah are commemorated in the roll of the faithful.

But then there was Isaac's son, Jacob. Like his grandfather Abraham, Jacob was a towering figure in Hebrew legend and tradition. After a rather spotty youth and a series of shabby episodes of selfishness and deceit, Jacob had matured into a man of disciplined discernment. He underwent a change of name to indicate his change of heart and life. From Jacob, "the Supplanter," he became Israel, "Preserver with God." So great was his influence on subsequent history that the name Israel came to designate his entire nation.

Abraham and Jacob, with Isaac in between. Two towering figures, Abraham and Jacob, and then that rather colorless Isaac in between. Yet the ancient formula of the Hebrew faith refers to the "God of Abraham, Isaac, and Jacob." Strange! He is right in there, right in there with his father, Abraham, and his son Jacob, both of whom come through as men of far greater accomplishments. And when the roll is called by the author of the Letter to the Hebrews—"By faith Abel offered to God a more acceptable sacrifice . . . By faith Enoch was taken up . . . By faith Noah, being warned by God . . . took heed and constructed an ark . . . By faith Abraham obeyed when he was called; and he went out . . . By faith Sarah herself received power to conceive . . . By faith Isaac . . ."[3]—Isaac is right in there with Abraham and Jacob and Moses and Joseph and all the rest of them. I am glad he is there, because he is such an ordinary man.

We know how it is. We go to church, we hear a sermon—
Martin Luther, John Wesley, Albert Schweitzer, extolled as ex-
amples for us. We are exhorted to that kind of faith in life. But
we sink back in our pews and think how we are not really Luthers
or Wesleys or Schweitzers. We could not start a Reformation or
go to Africa if we wanted to. We are bound into the place that
we occupy in our office or our profession or the home that we
run. Is God only the God of the Schweitzers and the Wesleys
and the Luthers, the Abrahams and the Jacobs? Are these the
ones with whom he is concerned? And then, we come across that
formula of Hebrew faith still used today, "the God of Abraham,
Isaac, and Jacob." Isaac is right in there, as an ordinary man.

As a matter of fact, Isaac shows up as a little less than ordinary upon occasion. He was a pushed-around man. He did not
even choose his own wife. The storyteller records: "Now Abraham was old, well advanced in years; and the LORD had blessed
Abraham in all things. And Abraham said to his servant, the
oldest in his house, who had charge of all that he had, 'Put your
hand under my thigh, and I will make you swear by the LORD,
the God of heaven and of the earth, that you will not take a wife
for my son from the daughters of the Canaanites, among whom
I dwell, but will go to my country and to my kindred, and take
a wife for my son Isaac.' " [4]

The servant went, and he came back with a woman named
Rebekah, the daughter of Bethuel, son of Milcah, wife of Abraham's brother Nahor. She proved a good choice in many ways,
but she was a manipulating woman and Isaac was a manipulatable
man. She played favorites between her twin sons, Jacob and
Esau. But then, so did Isaac. It is written: "When the boys
grew up, Esau was a skilful hunter, a man of the field, while
Jacob was a quiet man, dwelling in tents. Isaac loved Esau, because he ate of his game; but Rebekah loved Jacob." [5]

They were twins, but Esau was the elder by a few minutes
and that carried with it, in the Hebrew tradition, certain privi-
leges. However, Jacob was trickier than Esau, and with Rebekah,
his mother, by his side, he deceived his father on more than one

occasion. He even secured the much coveted older son's blessing, which should have gone to Esau.

Then, there is another series of episodes recorded in the life of Isaac. There was a famine in the land in which he lived. Isaac, with his family and all his people, went down to Abimelech, the Philistine king at Gerar. He lived there under Abimelech's protection. But as Isaac began to prosper, the Philistines were envious of his flocks and of his herds and of his slaves. So they stopped the wells that Abraham had dug and caused a water shortage. Isaac simply redug the old wells. But the trouble did not go away.

"And Abimelech said to Isaac, 'Go away from us; for you are much mightier than we.' So Isaac departed from there, and encamped in the valley of Gerar and dwelt there. And Isaac dug again the wells of water which had been dug in the days of Abraham his father; for the Philistines had stopped them after the death of Abraham; and he gave them the names which his father had given them. But when Isaac's servants dug in the valley and found there a well of springing water, the herdsmen of Gerar quarreled with Isaac's herdsmen, saying, 'The water is ours.' So he called the name of the well Esek, because they contended with him. Then they dug another well, and they quarreled over that also; so he called its name Sitnah. And he moved from there and dug another well, and over that they did not quarrel; so he called its name Rehoboth, saying, 'For now the LORD has made room for us, and we shall be fruitful in the land.' " [6]

We could call Isaac a peace-loving kind of individual and give him credit for refusing to get involved in warfare over water rights. But he did get pushed around now and then.

There is not much else you can say about him. A far smaller cluster of tales is gathered about the name of Isaac than about the name of his illustrious father, Abraham, or his distinguished son Jacob. He was a kind of connecting-link man, a connecting link between those two great makers of history. As such, maybe he is a symbol of sorts, a symbol of all the ordinary, connecting-link men and women who hold the world together between heroes. Isaac was no hero. He just went about his business, but God had

an eye out for him. After the episode with Abimelech, Isaac kept
on moving, searching for a place to settle. "From there he went
up to Beersheba. And the LORD appeared to him the same night
and said, 'I am the God of Abraham your father; fear not, for
I am with you and will bless you and multiply your descendants
for my servant Abraham's sake.' " [7]

He even impressed his old enemy, Abimelech. "Then Abimelech went to him from Gerar with Ahuzzath his adviser and Phicol
the commander of his army. Isaac said to them, 'Why have you
come to me, seeing that you hate me and have sent me away from
you?' They said, 'We see plainly that the LORD is with you; so
we say, let there be an oath between you and us, and let us make
a covenant with you, that you will do us no harm, just as we have
not touched you and have done to you nothing but good and have
sent you away in peace. You are now the blessed of the LORD.'
So he made them a feast, and they ate and drank. In the morning they rose early and took oath with one another; and Isaac set
them on their way, and they departed from him in peace." [8] Give
him credit. In a warring age, he was a man of peace. Maybe we
need more men like that.

I am all for the heroes, for the great men who arise in times
of crisis and fling their shadows across the future. And I am not
romanticizing the average man. I am just suggesting that between
heroes we need men and women who do not leave monuments
behind them, but who matter terribly in holding the whole together. Being a hero is a tiring business. Being a connecting-link
person, a holder-together of things, can be tiring also, and the re-
wards are not nearly as great. Isaac would never have made the
pages of history had he not been the son of Abraham and the
father of Jacob. But I am glad that he is there.

He represents a kind of continuity with the past. The only
sermons I have ever heard preached or have read about Isaac
took a text from Genesis 26:18, which reads: ". . . Isaac dug
again the wells of water which had been dug in the days of Abraham his father . . . and he gave them the names which his father
had given them." The point of the sermon usually is that Isaac's

act was that of a conservative man who realized the importance of old values and who was willing to re-dig old wells. Now, that is pushing the text a bit. I suppose it is essentially valid, but it is not the important thing. True, Abraham was a pioneer, Isaac was a settler. Abraham was an adventurer, Isaac was a consolidator. But to speak of this sense of continuity with the past, which he manifests, is not to make of him one of those stubborn persons who digs in his heels and rejects the world as it is. He did not try to turn the clock back. His father had left Ur of the Chaldees for unknown territory. There is no evidence that Isaac had any tendency to try to go back to Ur, to migrate once more to the old country. When I speak of him as a consolidator, I intend to convey the image of a man who set down roots where he was in order to maintain continuity with what had been. And that is important. Dag Hammarskjöld has written of his father: "He achieved an inner unity because, in the period of revolutionary development through which he lived, he remained faithful to his past, and faithful also to the past of others." [9] That kind of inner unity enables a man to maintain his balance in days of imbalance, to keep his identity in days when identity is threatened, to know who he is when things go awry. That kind of inner unity is so often lacking in our world. We are marked, many of us, either by frantic unreal devotion to a past that maybe never was or by passionate rejection of a past we do not understand. Yet we cannot know who we are unless we know whence we came. There is grace in a sense of identity that comes from knowing our roots.

On the other hand, we cannot know who we are without some vision of the future. Note this verse in the eleventh chapter of Hebrews: "By faith Isaac invoked future blessings on Jacob and Esau." [10] He thrust toward tomorrow. He maintained his continuity not only with what had been but with what was yet to be. In his own way, he was a voyager like his father on unknown seas, an explorer of lands not yet known, a seeker for a city yet to be found. In his own way, he was a man of faith. Any man or woman who maintains faithfulness in the present out of an acceptance of the past and a confidence in the future is worthy of note. Isaac deserves an appreciative word. Any man discerning

enough to salvage the values of yesterday while waiting expect-
antly and with openness for the values of tomorrow deserves an
appreciative word.

I think it all adds up to a commitment of life not *to* the
present, but *in* the present. So many of us live in a vacuum of
detachment. Thus we lack support at the critical points of our
existence. We lived bored, frustrated, lonely lives, emptied of
excitement and of meaning, and therefore we seek excitement.
Time hangs heavy on our hands. Viktor Frankl identifies what he
calls the "Sunday neurosis," which he describes as "that kind of
depression which afflicts people who become aware of the lack
of content in their lives when the rush of the busy week is over
and the void within themselves becomes manifest." [11] Not even
Sunday sports can cure the "Sunday neurosis" or fill the vacuum
of an empty life. Where do we find the framework into which our
ordinary experiences can fit? For most of life is ordinary, is it
not? For most of life is, as a woman told her psychiatrist, "so
terribly daily." It consists of handling the same routines, meeting
the same people, dealing with the same claims upon our time,
day by day, day by day, day by day. Most of us—most of the
time, at least—live Isaac-type lives, putting things in place, re-
digging old wells. Few of us are heroes. Most of us live between
Abraham and Jacob.

The man named Isaac was pretty faithful, but not always. He
had his bad moments. He lied to save his own skin. He played
favorites between his sons. But he was pretty faithful, and that
is the most you can say of most men.

Before he gave his full time to the writing of fiction, author
Lloyd C. Douglas was a parson in various cities of the United
States and, finally, in Montreal, Canada. He preached a sermon
in his Montreal church years ago in which he said this: ". . . sometimes I think we would do better—in our presentation of the
gospel—if we left off, for a little while, our eulogy of it as a
thing that came in, with a burst of celestial song and a blaze of
celestial starlight—and reached its climax in a heartrending tragedy—and just talk about what it will do to and for ordinary people, who are not deciding whether to go out the Via Dolorosa to

execution, but are wanting some good formula for helping them remember that there are sixteen ounces in a pound—when the competitor across the street has tinkered with his scales—for helping people to chasten their hair-trigger tempers; and empty their minds of desires for revenge; and cleanse them of their lusts, their greeds, their envies, their scramble to outdo their neighbors." [12] There is wisdom in that. At times, most of us need a formula to enable us just to hang in there.

This story is about Isaac, son of laughter. He opened no new frontiers. He spent his life milling around in the territory his father had already explored. He backed off from controversy. An ordinary man, a man who held things together. But God had an eye out for him and understood his frailty. The story affirms that, and that is important. The God of Abraham, Isaac, and Jacob knows who we are and understands where we can go and what we can do.

The Problems of Ordinary People

Once upon a time there was a man named Moses, a towering figure of a man. He was no ordinary man, but a changer of things, a monumental figure, one of those individuals who comes along maybe once in a century—or even less than that.

There was a man named Moses, who may or may not have looked like Charlton Heston. We cannot document that any more than we can document others of the legends and stories that rose about his name, for he was the kind of man about whom legends rise. We can document his importance, as Oesterley and Robinson have said in their *Hebrew Religion:* ". . . if we had no record of Moses, it would have been necessary to invent him, for such a work as that ascribed to him demands the genius and inspiration of an individual almost unique." [1]

Moses was a hero. Even his infancy is surrounded with an aura of wonder. Because the Hebrew tribes had multiplied to the point where they were threatening to their masters, the Egyptians, the reigning Pharaoh ". . . commanded all his people, 'Every son that is born to the Hebrews you shall cast into the Nile, but you shall let every daughter live.'

"Now a man from the house of Levi went and took to wife a daughter of Levi. The woman conceived and bore a son; and when she saw that he was a goodly child, she hid him three months. And when she could hide him no longer she took for him a basket made of bulrushes, and daubed it with bitumen and pitch; and she put the child in it and placed it among the reeds at the river's brink. And his sister stood at a distance, to know what would be done to him. Now the daughter of Pharaoh came down to bathe at the river, and her maidens walked beside the river; she saw the basket among the reeds and sent her maid to fetch it. When she opened it she saw the child; and lo, the babe was crying. She took pity on him and said, 'This is one of the Hebrews' children.' Then his sister said to Pharaoh's daughter, 'Shall I go and call you a nurse from the Hebrew women to nurse the child for you?' And Pharaoh's daughter said to her, 'Go.' So the girl went and called the child's mother. . . . And the child grew, and she brought him to Pharaoh's daughter, and he became her son; and she named him Moses, for she said, 'Because I drew him out of the water.' "² This kind of miracle story in ancient traditions is told only of mountain movers. Moses was a mountain mover.

The child of the bulrushes grew up. "One day, when Moses had grown up, he went out to his people and looked on their burdens; and he saw an Egyptian beating a Hebrew, one of his people. He looked this way and that, and seeing no one he killed the Egyptian and hid him in the sand." ³

This act of violent identification with his people, as "he looked on their burdens," was to mark the whole life of the man named Moses. His rash impulsive act on behalf of a slave led to his flight from the sheltered environs of the palace of the Pharaoh to the bleak hills of the land of Midian where he became a keeper of sheep. There he married the daughter of the priest of Midian. The day he went out and looked on the burden of his people was a life-changing day.

In Midian, a second life-changing event occurred. Here is how it happened: "Now Moses was keeping the flock of his father-in-law, Jethro, the priest of Midian; and he led his flock to the west side of the wilderness, and came to Horeb, the mountain of God. And the angel of the LORD appeared to him in a flame of fire out of the midst of a bush, and he looked, and lo, the bush was burning, yet it was not consumed. And Moses said, 'I will turn aside and see this great sight, why the bush is not burnt.' When the LORD saw that he turned aside to see, God called to him out of the bush, 'Moses, Moses!' And he said, 'Here am I.' Then he said, 'Do not come near; put off your shoes from your feet, for the place on which you are standing is holy ground.' And he said, 'I am the God of your father, the God of Abraham, the God of Isaac, and the God of Jacob.' And Moses hid his face, for he was afraid to look at God." [4]

There is something awe-inspiring still in that simple tale of the day when he was minding his flock and a voice spoke to him from a wayside bush. What happened? Not something you could take a picture of. You cannot make movies of an experience like that, as Hollywood has tried to do, and reproduce the flaming bush all lit up like a Christmas tree. No, whatever happened on that lonely, faraway hill was an inward transforming event, not an outward spectacle. Whatever happened was of monumental significance. This event turned the world on its axis. It still represents the final reality. It is one of those recurring occasional times when we, all of a sudden, realize that the ground on which we stand, the very ground, is holy, and we must take off our shoes in the presence of God—those occasional times when the sacred dimension of life bursts in upon us.

A speculative question such as "Does God exist?" is abstract and rather meaningless. Suppose you could *prove* an affirmative answer to the question, "Does God exist?" You could still walk away unmoved, untouched. But when you ask the question, "Is there a God who has dealings with me?" and by extension, "with my world?" then you move upon an entirely different level of reality. You are really asking if there is a grace-filling power for life. To that question some response is necessary. Moses found it so: "Then Moses said to God, 'If I come to the people of Israel and say to them, "The God of your fathers has sent me to you," and they ask me, "What is his name?" what shall I say to them?' God said to Moses, 'I AM WHO I AM.' " [5]

When God bursts in upon a person, he must make some response to him. Once we hear the name of God in personalized terms, once he becomes more than a great, abstract first cause, we are confronted with the necessity for some decision. "I AM WHO I AM," said the voice to Moses. And because that was said, never again could Moses quietly tend his sheep, detached and unconcerned. Such is the impact of the actuality of the God who says "I AM" to the human spirit. No longer an abstract idea to be argued about and discussed and discarded, God says, "I AM

WHO I AM. You are who you are. Respond!" Hear that? And the ground on which we stand is holy ground.

Once upon a time there was a man named Moses who, in the desert, brooded upon his people's burdens, and the act of murder that led to his flight, brooded as he tended his sheep and wandered the hillsides of Midian. And God came alive, became a named one. God comes alive to men in their experiences, not to trees and stones. It is true that the experience of Moses brought his memories, brought his past, his sense of identification, to that experience. He saw a bush burning, but it was *Moses, a man,* who saw it, the same Moses who was guilty of the crime of murder, the same Moses who had looked upon his kinsmen with compassion, the same Moses who had fled but who could not leave himself behind.

Stephen, in Joyce's *Ulysses,* says: "We walk through ourselves, meeting robbers, ghosts, giants, old men, young men, wives, widows, brothers-in-love. But always meeting ourselves." [6] And in meeting ourselves, bushes burn and a voice says, "I AM WHO I AM. You are who you are." God always moves into our lives at the deep places where we are who we are, where we are most ourselves with our hopes and our memories, our guilts and our failures, our fears and our anticipations. Moses had left the land of Egypt but he carried with him all of those experiences which could never be left behind. They were part of him forever.

When God spoke to him, he spoke to him in terms of Egypt, in terms of his memories. "Then the LORD said, 'I have seen the affliction of my people who are in Egypt, and have heard their cry because of their taskmasters; I know their sufferings, and I have come down to deliver them out of the hand of the Egyptians, and to bring them up out of that land to a good and broad land, a land flowing with milk and honey . . . And now, behold, the cry of the people of Israel has come to me, and I have seen the oppression with which the Egyptians oppress them. Come, I will send you to Pharaoh that you may bring forth my people, the sons of Israel out of Egypt.' "[7]

Note those words to Moses: "I have seen the affliction of my people . . . I have heard their cry . . . I have come down." The

Old Testament is replete with this kind of picture language concerning a God who hears the cries of troubled people and takes heed and comes down. He came down before the Flood. He came down to hear the strident cries of men at the Tower of Babel. He came down to Sinai. He keeps coming down.

This notion of the God who comes down is startling and, if we think upon it, a bit unsettling. For then we ask, Is he still the God who comes down? When does he come down? Does he come in judgment wherever wrong is done? Does he still hear the cries of all people in their misery? Or just sometimes? Does he hear our cries but not the cries of the refugees in war-torn countries? Whose cries does he hear? Is he no longer concerned with the miserable and the hurting? Is our commitment made to a God who just does not care? Or cares only for certain people?

Golfer Lee Trevino, after the British Open in 1972, said in that flippant way of his, "God must be a Mexican." Well, no, but some people take that kind of attitude toward God seriously. To assume such an attitude is not only to deny the God of the Old Testament but to deny the New Testament as well. The Christian doctrine of life centers upon the concept of the incarnation of God in Jesus Christ our Lord, which is but an expansion and refinement of the coming-down God who so loved the world.

Once upon a time there was a man named Moses and a God who said, "I AM WHO I AM," and the world was turned and a new vision came into being. And when the story of mankind is written, always high on the list of those who have made that story what it is, the name of Moses must be recorded. He gave men a new vision of freedom and ethical commitment. But then, to complete his story, it must be said that he died in keen personal disappointment. Being a hero is not necessarily a happy business. Heroes have all the problems of ordinary people.

There are few more touching scenes anywhere in literature than that story of the death of Moses in the book of Deuteronomy. "And the LORD said to Moses that very day, 'Ascend this mountain of the Abarim, Mount Nebo, which is in the land of Moab, opposite Jericho; and view the land of Canaan, which I give to the people of Israel for a possession; and die on the mountain which you ascend, and be gathered to your people, as Aaron your brother died in Mount Hor and was gathered to his people . . . For you shall see the land before you; but you shall not go there, into the land which I give to the people of Israel.' . . .

"And Moses went up from the plains of Moab to Mount Nebo, to the top of Pisgah, which is opposite Jericho. And the LORD showed him all the land, Gilead as far as Dan, all Naphtali, the land of Ephraim and Manesseh, all the land of Judah as far as the Western Sea, the Negeb, and the Plain, that is, the valley of Jericho the city of palm trees, as far as Zoar. And the LORD said to him, 'This is the land of which I swore to Abraham, to Isaac, and to Jacob, "I will give it to your descendants." I have let you see it with your eyes, but you shall not go over there.' So Moses the servant of the LORD died there in the land of Moab, according to the word of the LORD, and he buried him in the valley in the land of Moab opposite Bethpeor; but no man knows the place of his burial to this day. Moses was a hundred and twenty years old when he died; his eye was not dim, nor his natural force abated. And the people of Israel wept for Moses in the plains of Moab thirty days; then the days of weeping and mourning for Moses were ended.

". . . there has not arisen a prophet since in Israel like Moses, whom the LORD knew face to face, none like him for all the signs and the wonders which the LORD sent him to do in the land of Egypt, to Pharaoh and to all his servants and to all his land, and for all the mighty power and all the great and terrible deeds which Moses wrought in the sight of all Israel." [8]

Mighty Moses. Yet a man. No happy ending for him. He could not go over into the Promised Land. Why? He had failed to keep faith with his people on one traumatic occasion, and the old rabbinical legend tells how Moses climbed the hill and asked God why he could not go on. 'You doubted me," said God, "and I forgave that, Moses. You doubted your own power to lead this people and I forgave that. But you lost faith in the people; therefore, you cannot enter the Promised Land." No happy ending. Even heroes have their troubles and their disappointments. Even heroes have their sins. Moses gave way to despair and defeatism. How like us heroes often are.

It is good to remember that the God of heroes is our God, too, the God who hears, who heeds, who comes down, who stands by man in his betrayals, his failures, his denials. Moses forgot that for a time, forgot that God came to him while he was a fugitive from a murder charge, and said, "Moses, I AM WHO I AM." It was understandable that Moses should forget. But it adds a touch of poignancy to the end of his story. Maybe it is to remind us that all men, heroes included, have their faults. All men, even heroes, need forgiveness and grace. All men, even heroes, need help. All men, even heroes, are just like the rest of us.

In Marc Connelly's *Green Pastures,* the climactic scene of the story of Moses occurs when he stands by a great rock on a hillside. There is a soft singing that dies away. The last of the marchers disappears into the distance, and Moses speaks as into the empty air: "Yere I is, Lawd. De chillun is goin' into de Promised Land." Then the stage directions read: "God enters from behind the hill. He walks to Moses, puts his hands on his shoulders." Moses says, "You's with me, ain't you, Lawd?" And God says, "Co'se I is." Then finally he says, "Come on, ol' man." The stage directions read: "They continue up the hill. The stage is darkened." [9] Can you not hear a jazz band playing "Just a Closer Walk with Thee"?

> I am weak but Thou art strong.
> O Lord, keep me from all wrong.
> I'll be satisfied as long
> As I walk. Let me walk with Thee.[10]

The last you see of Moses he is still walking with the God who said to him out of a bush, "I AM WHO I AM."

So There Are Giants Ahead

Once upon a time there was a man named Joshua, and he stood straight and tall and sturdy among his people. "Joshua fit de battle of Jericho, And de walls come tumbling down." But there is more to his story than the story of that legendary battle. In Hebrew, the name Joshua means "Jahweh saves." In Greek, the name Joshua transliterated is the name Jesus. So, if you are writing "Jesus of Nazareth" in Hebrew, you write "Joshua of Nazareth." If you are writing in Greek, you write "Jesus, son of Nun," for the Joshua of legendary fame.

"Jahweh saves." In ancient times, names were intended to reflect character and identity. Joshua was one who saved his people in a time of particular crisis. He is a vague figure as far as facts go, by and large. The details of his life are few in the ancient narratives. He does come through in tradition as the successor of Moses after Moses' death. He assumed the role of leader after Moses died on the very edge of the land of Canaan. According to the story, it was Joshua who pulled together that motley band of desert nomads into at least a semblance of a fighting army, and moved against that equally motley collection of tribes west of the Jordan River.

Once upon a time there was a man named Joshua. He was a man of battle. He was a conqueror, resolute and strong. "After the death of Moses the servant of the LORD, the LORD said to Joshua the son of Nun, Moses' minister, 'Moses my servant is dead; now therefore arise, go over this Jordan, you and all this people, into the land which I am giving to them, to the people of Israel. Every place that the sole of your foot will tread upon I have given to you, as I promised to Moses. From the wilderness and this Lebanon as far as the great river, the river Euphrates, all the land of the Hittites to the Great Sea toward the going down of the sun shall be your territory. No man shall be able to stand before you all the days of your life; as I was with Moses, so I will be with you; I will not fail you or forsake you. Be strong and of good courage; for you shall cause this people to inherit the land which I swore to their fathers to give them.' " [1]

This was what Joshua heard. For Joshua, Jahweh was the Lord of hosts, the war-God of trumpet and of storms.

> Joshua fit de battle of Jericho,
> Jericho, Jericho,
> Joshua fit de battle of Jericho,
> And de walls come tumbling down.

The law of "herem" prevailed—that primitive code whereby an enemy population was placed under a ban, condemned to total destruction in the name of a deity. ". . . the people went up into the city, every man straight before him, and they took the city. Then they utterly destroyed all in the city, both men and women, young and old, oxen, sheep, and asses, with the edge of the sword." [2]

Sounds almost contemporary, does it not? Fleming James writes: "Here for the first time we meet with this terrible religious custom [herem], and we ought to pause a moment to consider its meaning. To destroy all living things and all valuable property in a conquered town was regarded as a specially meritorious act, for thereby the victors were renouncing in favour of the god all the spoils that they might otherwise take to themselves. But there was more in the transaction than renunciation. It was thought to gratify deity. Mesha of Moab, in his famous Moabite Stone, speaks of his killing the inhabitants of a captured town as a sight 'pleasing to Chemosh' (his god)." [3]

Herem was a harsh, cruel taboo, and efforts to justify it in the name of purity of religion ring hollow to us. But Joshua was a child of his age. It was a barbaric age, an age of primitive brutality. His vision of God was limited. What he thought he heard from God was strained through his own understanding. He was a conquerer. I guess the best you can say was that he was faithful to the vision he held. He clung to that vision loyally. He led his people by it, from the beginning to the end of his life. Perhaps the most significant accomplishment comes at the end of the book of Joshua.

"Then Joshua gathered all the tribes of Israel to Shechem . . . and the officers of Israel; and they presented themselves before God. And Joshua said to all the people, 'Thus says the LORD, the God of Israel, "Your fathers lived of old beyond the Euphrates, Terah, the father of Abraham and of Nahor; and they served other gods. Then I took your father Abraham from beyond the River and led him through all the land of Canaan, and made his offspring many. I gave him Isaac; and to Isaac I gave Jacob and Esau. . . . Then I brought your fathers out of Egypt, and you came to the sea; and the Egyptians pursued your fathers with chariots and horsemen to the Red Sea. . . .

" 'Now therefore fear the LORD, and serve him in sincerity and in faithfulness; put away the gods which your fathers served beyond the River, and in Egypt, and serve the LORD. . . . choose this day whom you will serve, whether the gods your fathers served in the region beyond the River, or the gods of the Amorites in whose land you dwell; but as for me and my house, we will serve the LORD. . . .'

"After these things Joshua the son of Nun, the servant of the LORD, died, being a hundred and ten years old." [4]

Joshua was a man of battle, a man of loyalty and commitment. But as a saint he is a bit of a problem. He was ruthless, the fanatical leader of a fanatical people. The best we can do with the problem is set it down in the place in history where it belongs. John Bright says of the Israelites: "For them the use of force to achieve the purpose of their God was justified." [5] It was acceptable in that time of primitive development. But to recognize their viewpoint does not mean approval by us or an example for us. It does not mean acceptance of primitive brutality or commitment to it as God's will and way in our time. It means an acknowledgment of the God who is God, the God of Amos and Isaiah, of Hosea, Jeremiah, and Jonah, and above all, the God of Jesus, that other "Joshua" of Nazareth. For if they are right, God must have loved the people of Jericho as well as the Israelites. To see Joshua in his historical context is to see a whole host of men and women throughout the centuries justifying their conquests in the name of God.

We cannot make Joshua more than he was. Nor, recognizing him as a child of his time, can we make him less than he was. He *was* a man of vision. He was a leader of incomparable valor and decisiveness. He was able to enter into the vacuum created by the death of Moses and to continue to lead that ragtag and bobtail conglomeration of desert tribes called the Hebrews into the land of Canaan and leave there the beginnings, at least, of a great nation. He was able to transfer vision to them, able to draw them into a circle of commitment to a purer view of God than prevailed in the tribes around them. He moved toward the kind of sustaining grace that upholds people in times of crisis.

Perhaps that incident recorded in the book of Numbers reflects the character and the nature of this man at an earlier stage, a character and nature that persevered through all of his experiences. According to the story, Moses selected twelve men and sent them to spy out the land of Canaan and to report their findings to the group. He said to them: " 'Go up into the Negeb yonder, and go up into the hill country, and see what the land is, and whether the people who dwell in it are strong or weak, whether they are few or many, and whether the land that they dwell in is good or bad . . . and whether there is wood in it or not. Be of good courage, and bring some of the fruit of the land.' . . .

"So they went up and spied out the land from the wilderness of Zin to Rehob, near the entrance of Hamath. . . . And they came to the valley of Eshcol, and cut down from there a branch with a single cluster of grapes, and they carried it on a pole between two of them; they brought also some pomegranates and figs. . . .

"At the end of forty days they returned from spying out the land. And they came to Moses and Aaron and to all the congregation of the people of Israel in the wilderness of Paran, at Kadesh; they brought back word to them and to all the congregation, and showed them the fruit of the land. And they told him, 'We came to the land to which you sent us; it flows with milk and honey, and this is its fruit. Yet the people who dwell in the land are strong, and the cities are fortified and very large; and besides, we saw the descendants of Anak there. The Amalekites dwell in the land of the Negeb; the Hittites, the Jebusites, and the Amorites dwell in the hill country; and the Canaanites dwell by the sea, and along the Jordan.' "[6]

Their report was full of foreboding, tales of Amalekites and of Hittites and of Jebusites and of Amorites, and worst of all, of the sons of Anak. Anak means "long-necked." They were the long-necked, tall descendants of the legendary giants, these sons of Anak. And ten of the twelve spies were ready to abandon the whole project to avoid any further confrontation. But two of the twelve were of different caliber. One was the man Caleb, who was of the tribe of Judah.

"But Caleb quieted the people . . . and said, 'Let us go up at once, and occupy it; for we are well able to overcome it.' Then the men who had gone up with him said, 'We are not able to go up against the people; for they are stronger than we. . . . The land, through which we have gone, to spy it out, is a land that devours its inhabitants; and all the people that we saw in it are men of great stature. And there we saw the Nephilim (the sons of Anak, who come from the Nephilim); and we seemed to ourselves like grasshoppers, and so we seemed to them.' "[7] Then they all raised a loud cry, and they all wanted to go home.

Had they come this far to quit now, to give up, to go home? Had they come this far to forget the whole thing? It was a crucial moment for them. The leaders, Moses and Aaron, were aghast. They threw themselves on the ground in extravagant protest. Then Caleb came again, front and center, and with him the young man Joshua, son of Nun, an Ephraimite. They tore their clothes and said to the people, "The land, which we passed through to spy it out, is an exceedingly good land. If the LORD delights in us, he will bring us into this land and give it to us, a land which flows with milk and honey. . . . do not fear the people of the land, for they are bread for us; their protection is removed from them, and the LORD is with us; do not fear them."[8]

Caleb and Joshua, two against ten, two against the majority, none of whose names you would recognize were I to list them. There were ten men who explored the land and were afraid. They said, "We felt no bigger than grasshoppers." And then, there were two men who said, "Let us go up. We can do it."

Sadly enough, the people listened to the ten. They spent forty years wandering in the wilderness as a penalty for their fears, for they were afflicted with the grasshopper complex, the grasshopper complex of the ten. They said, "We seemed to ourselves . . ." That was how they viewed themselves. In the presence of giants they seemed to themselves like grasshoppers. A grasshopper does not cut much of a figure in nature. A grasshopper never knows when a giant foot will step down upon him and crush out his life. So the grasshopper keeps on the move but never gets anywhere. Those of us who think of ourselves as grasshoppers never get anywhere. Certainly, we never get to the land of the giants where the milk and honey are.

Men like Caleb and Joshua rise above the image of the grasshopper. They are ready to go on. Giants ahead? So there are giants ahead. Do not fear. There is little question where the future lies in periods of change and transition. The future lies with the Calebs and the Joshuas, not with those who see themselves as grasshoppers, those who denigrate themselves and denigrate mankind as a whole.

Joshua represents the visionary who seeks the land of milk and honey. The others, those nameless ten who represent the fearless, the cynical, the lazy, see only the giants. That difference of viewpoint determines events.

And there are giants out there today, looming over us, giants whose handprints are inked across the front page of every morning newspaper. There is a giant bitterness growing out of our unsolved racial tensions, tensions still remaining for many, the milk and honey of brotherhood way over the hill. There is the gaunt giant of poverty. There is the grim giant of a lawless disregard for the rules of conduct by which civilized men must live if they are to survive, rules without which a society will crack and break apart. There is the lurking giant of violence who erupts every now and then and stretches his muscles. There is the grinning giant of moral confusion and the sneering giant of corruption and decay of the very political processes by which we hang together. Giants all right! Sons of Anak, long-necked, fearsome, and grotesque.

But we are not grasshoppers. Beyond and even among the giants, there is the land of milk and honey, the vision and the dream by which men feed their hopes. The land of Canaan can only be entered by those who are willing to move beyond their fears and prejudices, their petty greeds. The promised land is only for men and women who, in the name of God, will shed their grasshopper complexes. Dag Hammarskjöld writes: "The work for security and freedom from fear . . . will prove hopeless . . . unless peoples and governments alike are willing to take immediate risks. This will give us a better chance to avoid the final disaster threatening us if we do not manage to turn the course of developments in a new direction." [9] This is a day, it would seem to me, for a recommitment to all that is best within us as a people. And for us in the church?

Well, once upon a time there was a man named Joshua son of Nun. And then, there was another man with the same name, Joshua of Nazareth. His vision was greater than that of Joshua son of Nun. Joshua son of Nun dreamed of the conquest of a land for his people. That other Joshua, the one we call Jesus, the one from Nazareth, dreamed not of conquest of anybody but of a brotherhood of men. Joshua son of Nun went forth with sword in hand to hew out a destiny. It was the best that he knew. Jesus of Nazareth went forth with nothing in his hand and carried a cross upon his back. Joshua son of Nun changed the story of his people. Jesus of Nazareth changed the history of mankind. Joshua son of Nun—we call him brave, valiant, a leader of men. Jesus of Nazareth—we call him Lord and Master. It is Jesus of Nazareth whom we follow, whose courage inspires us to confront the giants which are ahead.

The King Arthur of Jewish History

Once upon a time there was a man named David and he was a king. That is not all he was. He was a shepherd, a soldier, a part-time musician and poet, a hired mercenary, and for a while, a full-time brigand. He had a variety of careers and he seemed to do well in all of them. He did so well as king that he became a symbol of Israel's Golden Age. According to the book of Samuel, God promised an everlasting dynasty to the house of David. "Your house and your kingdom shall be made sure forever before me; your throne shall be established forever." [1] When difficulties came and adversities fell upon the people of Israel, her poets and prophets were apt to beseech God that he would redeem his promise to the house of David. In the time of Jesus, the common rabbinic teaching was that the Messiah would come from the royal line of David. That is why the New Testament writer stressed the ancestry of Jesus as traceable to David himself.

David threw a long shadow across the history of his people. We meet him first as a shepherd boy who won the favor of the king, Saul. It is a romantic story. There was a lad, a keeper of sheep. Tradition has it that he was the youngest of eight sons of Jesse, all of them vigorous and virile men. It was said of David that he was "ruddy and had beautiful eyes and was handsome." One account of the way he came to the notice of the king is connected with one of Saul's periodic depressions. "So Saul said to his servants, 'Provide for me a man who can play well, and bring him to me.' One of the young men answered, 'Behold, I have seen a son of Jesse the Bethlehemite, who is skilful in playing, a man of valor, a man of war, prudent in speech, and a man of good presence; and the LORD is with him.' Therefore Saul sent messengers to Jesse and said, 'Send me David your son, who is with the sheep.' . . . [And Jesse sent him.] And Saul loved him greatly, and he become his armor-bearer. . . . And whenever the evil spirit from God was upon Saul, David took the lyre and played it with his hand; so Saul was refreshed, and was well, and the evil spirit departed from him." [2]

Then, there is a different account which is woven into the narrative of Samuel of a day when the Philistines massed for war against the Israelites. "And there came out from the camp of the Philistines a champion named Goliath, of Gath, whose height was six cubits and a span. He had a helmet of bronze on his head, and he was armed with a coat of mail, and the weight of the coat was five thousand shekels of bronze. And he had greaves of bronze upon his legs, and a javelin of bronze slung between his shoulders. And the shaft of his spear was like a weaver's beam, and his spear's head weighed six hundred shekels of iron; and his shield-bearer went before him. He stood and shouted to the ranks of Israel, 'Why have you come out to draw up for battle? Am I not a Philistine, and are you not servants of Saul? Choose a man for yourselves, and let him come down to me. If he is able to fight with me and kill me, then we will be your servants; but if I prevail against him and kill him, then you shall be our servants and serve us.' And the Philistine said, 'I defy the ranks of Israel this day; give me a man, that we may fight together.' When Saul and all Israel heard these words of the Philistine, they were dismayed and greatly afraid." [3]

For forty days and forty nights he taunted them. Israel was immobilized by her fears. And then David, son of Jesse, was sent by Jesse to bring provisions for his brothers in the camp of Israel. When David arrived and heard the jeering words of Goliath, he was appalled that no man from Israel dared take arms against him who defied the armies of the living God.

"When the words which David spoke were heard, they repeated them before Saul; and he sent for him. And David said to Saul, 'Let no man's heart fail because of him; your servant will go and fight with this Philistine.' And Saul said to David, 'You are not able to go against this Philistine to fight with him; for you are but a youth, and he has been a man of war from his youth.' But David said to Saul, 'Your servant used to keep sheep for his father; and when there came a lion, or a bear, and took a lamb from the flock, I went after him and smote him and delivered it out of his mouth; and if he arose against me, I caught him by his beard, and smote him and killed him. Your servant has killed both lions and bears; and this uncircumcised Philistine shall be like one of them, seeing he has defied the armies of the living God.' And David said, 'The LORD who delivered me from the paw of the lion and from the paw of the bear, will deliver me from the hand of this Philistine.' And Saul said to David, 'Go, and the LORD be with you!' " [4]

So he went, rejecting the armor of the king and selecting five smooth stones from the brook with which he slew the Philistine. He was small but he was big enough for Goliath, the giant.

David became a man of mighty deeds and legendary valor. But David lost the favor of the king almost as quickly as he had gained it.

"As they were coming home, when David returned from slaying the Philistine, the women came out of all the cities of Israel, singing and dancing, to meet King Saul, with timbrels, with songs of joy, and with instruments of music. And the women sang to one another as they made merry. 'Saul has slain his thousands, and David his ten thousands.' And Saul was very angry, and this saying displeased him; he said, 'They have ascribed to David ten thousands, and to me they have ascribed thousands; and what more can he have but the kingdom?' And Saul eyed David from that day on." [5]

David was forced to flee from the presence of the king, and he took to the wilderness. There he molded an outlaw band which, as Fleming James says, became the "most effective fighting unit that Israel ever possessed, creating the nucleus of a future army which was to know no defeat." [6] Once upon a time there was a man named David, a man of mighty deeds and legendary valor.

He was a king, too, a king of vision and of statesmanship. After the death of Saul, David, at thirty-seven, became undisputed ruler of Israel. For thirty-three years he reigned. The boundaries of Israel were extended to their farthest extremity, her wealth enhanced to a greater degree than ever before, her foreign relationships strengthened by trade and tribute. It was the Golden Era for these tribes, loosely bound together by the name Hebrew. No wonder generations yet to come were to sing of the splendors of David and the glories of his kingdom. David was a king among kings.

David was a strange and complex man. His whole career is surrounded by an aura of romance, his legendary exploits set in an atmosphere of fantasy. He was the King Arthur of Jewish history. The Camelot of his reign was Jerusalem. But throughout all his career there are interwoven strands of barbarism and civilization. He was a tender lover of women and a stalwart friend of men. Yet, he was as brutal as any brigand, as untrustworthy as any outlaw. While fleeing Saul, he sought refuge among the Philistines and the protection of their king, Achish. He raided the allies of the Philistines. And, as the storyteller says, "left neither man nor woman alive, but took away the sheep, the oxen, the asses, the camels, and the garments, and come back to Achish." [7]

When he was asked what he had done, he lied and told Achish that he had fought against the tribes of Judah. "Such was his custom all the while he dwelt in the country of the Philistines. And Achish trusted David." [8]

This is the same man to whom is attributed the lines of the twenty-third Psalm. What a strange and contradictory character! He could dance in ecstasy before the ark of Jahweh and plunge into battle with the ferocity of a lion. He slew two hundred Philistines to gain the hand of Michal, the daughter of King Saul. Then, when he was forced to leave the palace of Saul, he left Michal behind but he did not forget her. When later, Abner, Saul's general, sought to make peace with David after the death of Saul, there was one condition David insisted upon—that Abner not come back into his presence without bringing his beloved Michal. And yet, not long after that, because of a taunt, he put her aside and she died childless and rejected and alone. What an odd mixture of savagery and chivalry.

He was a warrior king who could not manage his own household. He had more trouble with his children than any man ought to have. Their lives were marred by deeds of rape, of incest, of fratricide and attempted patricide. There was his beloved Absalom who led a revolt against his own father, so that David was forced to flee the capital city. And when the revolt was quelled and the news came of the death of Absalom, David wept. It is one of the most poignant expressions in all of literature: "O my son Absalom, my son, my son Absalom! Would I had died instead of you, O Absalom, my son, my son!" [9]

What a strange mixture of man David was. A despot who could accept rebuke and acknowledge wrongdoing, and repent. Perhaps the darkest and best-known chapter of his life concerns a faithful soldier named Uriah and Uriah's wife, Bathsheba. It is a tale of lust and treachery. From the rooftop of the palace, David had beheld Bathsheba at her bath. In typical despotic fashion, he had sent for her and taken her into the palace. When she became pregnant, he tried craftily to shift the responsibility to her husband, Uriah, who was with the army in the field. When craft failed, he took more direct and brutal steps, having Uriah put in an exposed position in battle, abandoned, and killed by the enemy. Then he married Bathsheba.

But Israel was not without its outspoken prophet, a man named Nathan. "And the LORD sent Nathan to David. He came to him, and said to him, 'There were two men in a certain city, the one rich and the other poor. The rich man had very many flocks and herds; but the poor man had nothing but one little ewe lamb, which he had bought. And he brought it up, and it grew up with him and with his children; it used to eat of his morsel, and drink from his cup, and lie in his bosom, and it was like a daughter to him. Now there came a traveler to the rich man, and he was unwilling to take one of his own flock or herd to prepare for the wayfarer who had come to him, but he took the poor man's lamb, and prepared it for the man who had come to him.' Then David's anger was greatly kindled against the man; and he said to Nathan, 'As the LORD lives, the man who has done this deserves to die; and he shall restore the lamb fourfold, because he did this thing, and because he had no pity.'

"Nathan said to David, 'You are the man.' . . . David said to Nathan, 'I have sinned against the LORD.' " [10]

Centuries later Paul, addressing some Jews in Antioch of Pisidia, reviews the highlights of Israel's history and reminds them of Samuel, the great prophet, and of Saul, son of Kish. And then there are these words: ". . . he raised up David to be their king; of whom he testified and said, 'I have found in David the son of Jesse a man after my heart, who will do all my will.' " [11]

Well, what do you think of that? Outlaw, liar, revolutionist, murderer, adulterer—"a man after my heart"? What can that mean? It turns all our ways of evaluating conduct upside down, doesn't it? Did not God know about David? How did he fit in? David certainly was not a good man as we count goodness much of the time. Why was it written of him, the only Biblical character of whom it is written, a man after God's own heart?

Maybe it was his honesty. When he was confronted with his own evil, he did not justify it or rationalize it or whine about it. When Nathan came to him with his story and David heard him out, he did not equivocate or call his sin other than what it was. He did not say, "But you do not understand the pressures I was under." He said simply and directly, "I have sinned."

Or maybe it was the heart of him, the tenderness that marked him. He was, as I have said, a tender lover of women and a stalwart friend of men. He was big and magnanimous. He was a lover of Michal and Bathsheba and Absalom and Saul, the king, even after Saul had turned against him. Once, while David was hiding in a cave from the vengeance of Saul, Saul himself entered the cave but did not see David and his men in the darkness. David's men saw their chance and placed their hands on their swords, but David persuaded them not to attack. He cut off a fragment of Saul's garment. Then, after Saul had gone a safe distance, David called to him and said, "See, see."

When Saul was slain, David lamented:

> Thy glory, O Israel, is slain upon thy high places!
>   How are the mighty fallen!
> Tell it not in Gath,
>   publish it not in the streets of Ashkelon . . .[12]

He loved Saul. He loved Jonathan, Saul's son, his friend. Though forced by the exigencies of politics to separate from each other, they never lost their feeling for each other. And over Jonathan's fallen body David keened his lament:

> How are the mighty fallen
> in the midst of the battle!
>
> Jonathan lies slain upon thy high places.
> I am distressed for you, my brother Jonathan;
> very pleasant have you been to me;
> your love to me was wonderful,
> passing the love of women.[13]

Maybe his secret was the magnanimity of his spirit. The author of First Peter was to write, "Love covers a multitude of sins." [14] And one day Jesus, eating in the house of a Pharisee, watched a woman creep in and weep over him, wetting his feet with her tears, drying them with her hair, and anointing them with ointment. And when his dinner companion drew back in horror, he said, ". . . her sins, which are many, are forgiven, for she loved much . . ." [15] Maybe Franklin Roosevelt was right when he said that the sins of the warmhearted and the sins of the cold-blooded are weighed in different scales.

Maybe it was the way David kept coming back to God, throwing himself on God's grace over and over again. I know there is danger here, danger of what Bonhoeffer called "cheap grace." A cartoon, years ago, showed little George Washington standing there with his hatchet in his hand, saying, "I did it father, I chopped down the cherry tree with my little hatchet." And his father said, "All right, so you admit it. You *always* admit it. The question is, When are you going to stop doing it?" That is the question of true repentance. David did keep coming back, however. But he never made it to the level of sainthood. He lived with the demons of sensuality and deceit all his life, but he never finally abandoned himself to them. He kept struggling back. He kept holding to the God whose care he had trusted as a shepherd lad among the lions and the bears.

To him is attributed the fifty-first Psalm, supposedly written after the Bathsheba episode:

> Have mercy on me, O God,
>   according to thy steadfast love;
>   according to thy abundant mercy
>   blot out my transgressions.
> Wash me thoroughly from my iniquity,
>   and cleanse me from my sin![16]

Maybe God understood him better than we would. Queen Victoria once said primly and severely: "David is not a person with whom I should wish to associate." I guess not. He would have frightened her to death. But there he is in the Bible. There he is in the words of Paul—a man after God's own heart. There he is! Lynn Harold Hough says: ". . . so tender that he will not drink water brought to him by men who have secured it at the risk of their lives, so loyal that his friendship with Jonathan has become a perpetual lyric, so hot with passionate energy that he can turn utterly cruel at the command of lust, so honest with himself that his repentance is more terrible than the defeat of an army with banners. And in all his fierce, tempestuous, and powerful life he has one great and masterful companion, the Lordly Person whose character is his perpetual rebuke and yet, because he loves fully that which he only partly becomes, his perpetual glory." [17]

Once upon a time there was a man named David. He was a king, but that is not all. A great rogue, a great sinner, a great lover. Robin Hood of the wilderness, King Arthur in a desert Camelot. A singer of songs that are bittersweet. A poet whose ecstasy turns to prayer. Once there was a man named David, and it could be said of him, He was a man after God's own heart.

Protecting Ourselves from the Truth

Once upon a time there were two kings—Jehoshaphat, king of Judah, in the south, and Ahab, king of Israel, in the north. Ahab was not much, not even as kings go. He was dominated by his wife, Jezebel, whose very name has come to mean "wicked woman." She pushed him into all sorts of unfortunate alliances. But then, it must be confessed that Ahab was eminently pushable. He led Israel into idolatry as well as into unfortunate foreign entanglements. The chronicler of the book of Kings sums him up: "In the thirty-eighth year of Asa king of Judah, Ahab the son of Omri began to reign over Israel, and Ahab the son of Omri reigned over Israel in Samaria twenty-two years. And Ahab the son of Omri did evil in the sight of the LORD more than all that were before him." [1]

The other king, Jehoshaphat, was not bad as kings go. It was said of him: "Jehoshaphat the son of Asa began to reign over Judah in the fourth year of Ahab king of Israel. Jehoshaphat was thirty-five years old when he began to reign, and he reigned twenty-five years in Jerusalem. His mother's name was Azubah the daughter of Shilhi. He walked in all the way of Asa his father; he did not turn aside from it, doing what was right in the sight of the LORD; yet the high places were not taken away, and the people still sacrificed and burned incense on the high places. Jehoshaphat also made peace with the king of Israel." [2]

Now Jehoshaphat had his weaknesses. He was susceptible, apparently, to dreams of grandeur. Twice he entered into unwise alliances with other kings, and each time those alliances ended in catastrophe. Let us look at one of those disastrous ventures.

It all began when Jehoshaphat made a state visit to Ahab, king of Israel. Ahab and Israel were in a state of armed truce with the country of Syria, with whom Israel carried on inter-

77

mittent warfare throughout most of the ninth century, B.C. Ahab took advantage of Jehoshaphat's visit to suggest a military expedition against the border town of Ramoth-gilead, which the Syrians had seized from Israel a few years previously. Ahab asked Jehoshaphat to join in that expedition. Jehoshaphat was agreeable (for one of his weaknesses seems to have been a certain pliability). He responded to the invitation extravagantly. "I am as you are, my people as your people, my horses as your horses." [3] Then a note of caution entered in. "Inquire first for the word of the Lord." [4]

So Ahab summoned the whole ecclesiastical establishment, about four hundred court preachers. " 'Shall I go to battle against Ramoth-gilead, or shall I forbear?' And they said, 'Go up; for the LORD will give it into the hand of the king.' " [5]

Jehoshaphat was a cut above Ahab, as I have already indicated. He seems to have had more religious sensitivity and, perhaps, he was a bit shrewder. He looked over that motley conglomeration of kept preachers, of sleep-in prophets, and he was suspicious. So Jehoshaphat said: " 'Is there not here another prophet of the LORD of whom we may inquire?' And the king of Israel said to Jehoshaphat, 'There is yet one man by whom we may inquire of the LORD, Micaiah the son of Imlah; but I hate him, for he never prophesies good concerning me, but evil.' " [6]

Isn't that typical of us all? In one way or another we all try to protect ourselves against the unpleasantness of truth. Ahab had made up his mind to go to war. His advisers were wise enough to see that he had made up his mind and wise enough not to oppose him. They knew that his request for advice was really a request for approval. Ahab was sure of them; he paid them. But he was not sure of Micaiah. Did he want the truth? No, not unless the truth conformed to what he had already decided. He wanted corroboration of a previously arrived at decision. Ahab wanted his opinions confirmed. He wanted his decisions justified. His mind was set on war with Syria. He wanted Jehoshaphat to go with him, so he did not want to hear contrary opinions about his expedition.

Certainly, the story of political leaders from then until now illustrates this perennial quirk of human nature. It is startling today to see the emergence from oblivion of career diplomats who, thirty years ago, were telling the truth as they understood it about the great subcontinent of China. That truth then was contrary to the official cold-war position of our government in the 40's and 50's. So careers were blasted, reputations ruined, men sent into exile—not because what they said was refuted and proved wrong, but because what they said was unpleasant and contrary to official postures. The Marquis of Halifax once said: "Nothing has an uglier look to us than reason when it is not on our side."

So Ahab used the old point-the-finger-at-the-truth-teller trick. If you do not like what he says, hate him. The Romans had a phrase for it. They called it arguing "ad hominem," that is, directing your argument against the man, appealing to prejudices rather than to reason.

In all probability, Micaiah was a grumpy, unpleasant chap with rough edges, given to tactless approaches to people. "Prophets" usually are that way. The Old Testament is filled with tales of conflict between kings and prophets. The prophets, invariably, were outside the favored court circles. They did not mix well with the "in" group. They were blunt and fiercely independent. They were upsetters of the smooth order of things.

Micaiah was no exception to this categorization of prophets. He did not belong. He did not fit in with the four hundred court preachers whom Ahab kept close about him to pronounce benedictions upon his activities. The story of Micaiah is a brief one for this is his only appearance in all of the Bible and it was an unsuccessful appearance. He fades into obscurity after this incident. Who wants people like him around? Certainly, ambitious politicians do not. Micaiahs are too bothersome. So it is best to hate them, to destroy them, to point the finger of scorn at them. They can be labeled troublemakers, agitators, traitors, communists, anarchists. Anything! Thus their messages can be evaded. They do not have to be evaluated on their own merits. Their truth or falsity can be safely ignored. The easiest way to discredit unpleasant truths is to discredit the bearers of those truths.

Now, this kind of reaction is not confined to kings and politicians. This is a universal kind of reaction to things that threaten us and threaten our self-images. None of us likes to be confronted with that which contradicts what we have already decided about ourselves or about some situation. When our prejudices are threatened, we avoid the facts or the feelings that threaten those prejudices by attacking the person who presents the facts or feelings. Thus for a long time the civil rights movement, particularly in the South, was attributed to hated "outside agitators," until such a fantasy simply became no longer believable at all. Most of us did not want to accept that which attacked the basis of our inbred sense of racial superiority or our comfortable sense of the status quo. Our whole view of the nature of things, as those things should be, was threatened, and so our instinctive way of resisting change was to discredit the changers.

The problem with this kind of thing is that it does not work for very long. It did not work for Ahab. At Jehoshaphat's insistence, Micaiah was sent for. "And when he had come to the king, the king said to him, 'Micaiah, shall we go to Ramothgilead to battle, or shall we forbear?' And he answered him, 'Go up and triumph; the LORD will give it into the hand of the king.' "⁷ And Ahab knew that he was mocking him and that he was taunting those four hundred house parsons.

"But the king said to him, 'How many times shall I adjure you that you speak to me nothing but the truth in the name of the LORD?' And [Micaiah] said, 'I saw all Israel scattered upon the mountains, as sheep that have no shepherd; and the LORD said, "These have no master; let each return to his home in peace." ' And the king of Israel said to Jehoshaphat, 'Did I not tell you that he would not prophesy good concerning me, but evil?' "⁸ Ahab was justified. And the next step?

"And the king of Israel said, 'Seize Micaiah, and take him back to Amon the governor of the city and to Joash the king's son; and say, "Thus says the king, 'Put this fellow in prison, and feed him with scant fare of bread and water, until I come in peace.' " ' " [9]

So Ahab and Jehoshaphat went off to battle. And a certain man drew his bow at random, the arrow struck Ahab in the breast, and he died. The grim summary? "So the king died, and was brought to Samaria; and they buried the king in Samaria. And they washed the chariot by the pool of Samaria, and the dogs licked up his blood, and the harlots washed themselves in it, according to the word of the LORD which he had spoken. Now the rest of the acts of Ahab, and all that he did, and the ivory house which he built, and all the cities that he built, are they not written in the Book of the Chronicles of the Kings of Israel? So Ahab slept with his fathers; and Ahaziah his son reigned in his stead." [10]

Thus ends the saga of Ahab, and the brief account of Micaiah ends, too. What happened to him? Did he rot in jail? Did he die as punishment for what he had said? Did he go into hiding somewhere, into exile? Who knows? He just never shows up again.

Whatever happened to him, one thing is clear. You cannot avoid the truth by calling names and pointing fingers. Jehoshaphat and Ahab should have listened to Micaiah, but they did not. They wrecked themselves and they wrecked a kingdom. But, then, who does listen? Sad repetitions of history give an answer to that question. What, for example, did we learn from World War II? Winston Churchill once said: "The disproportion between the quarrels of nations and the suffering which fighting out those quarrels involves; the poor and barren prizes which reward sublime endeavor on the battlefield; the fleeting triumphs of war; the long, slow rebuilding; the awful risks so hardily run; the doom missed by a hair's breadth, by the spin of a coin, by the accident of an accident—all this should make the prevention of another great war the main preoccupation of mankind." [11] But it has not been; the arms race, renewed, has been. No wonder Churchill put as the theme of volume six of his *Second World War* this:

HOW THE GREAT DEMOCRACIES
TRIUMPHED,
AND SO WERE ABLE TO RESUME
THE FOLLIES
WHICH HAD SO NEARLY
COST THEM THEIR
LIFE[12]

What have we learned from Vietnam? Time will tell.

But who does listen to Micaiahs? Kings and princes aside, who listens on a personal and private level? Who listens to the person who threatens his preconceptions and self-complacency? Who listens when life's programs and purposes are questioned? Blunt honesty is seldom either accepted or appreciated. Yet is it not the beginning of salvation? The alcoholic begins the road back into sobriety when he gives up his defenses and listens to the truth about himself. Each of us needs some Micaiah now and then, some rough voice of judgment, even of condemnation. Each of us needs a Micaiah, a voice speaking to us and hurting us at times, telling the truth about ourselves.

Psychiatrist Eda LeShan tells of one night when she and her husband were trying to comfort their daughter after a nightmare and talk about the dark in realistic terms. "But I'm afraid of *my* dark," said the child. "And of course," writes Dr. LeShan, "that is the crux of the matter . . . Each of us has to face our 'own dark'—the dark side of man's nature." [13] It may be revealed by a voice in the temple, by the sobbed-out hurt of a loved one, by the angry estrangement of a friend, or even by a chance word, if we are open. But each of us has his own Micaiah to confront him. A place for conflict and appreciation of conflict belongs in every relationship.

Once upon a time there were two kings and a rough-tongued prophet. The kings had plotted a war and they wanted support. They got it from everyone but that rough-tongued prophet. Micaiah told the truth, as he understood it, and he went to jail. The two kings rejected the truth Micaiah understood and went to war and ended in catastrophe. What a story! And what do we do with it? Leave it there? There is no gospel in that, no news of redemption.

The first thrust of the gospel emphasis begins there, I think: the call to be honest, to be open, to repent, to look at ourselves. We do not like to hear rough voices, but it is part of the total story of the lives of all of us. Our first confrontation with Christ may bring the tones of Micaiah.

The second thrust of the gospel is to push us on toward the Resurrection, toward the healing and liberating Christ, toward the living Christ and the surrounding grace, toward the laughter at the heart of life, and the forgiveness at the center of God's reaching-out heart. With that we can face our Micaiahs and be honest about ourselves. We can listen even to judgment, because the voice of judgment has in it more than doom. It has in it hope and restoration.

So the two thrusts merge, at last, into one. And in confrontation with Christ, we are secure enough to accept judgment, because mixed with it is the word of forgiveness, and reaching through it to us is the gentle hand of God's reconciliation and peace.

Wisdom No One Wants

Once upon a time there was a man named Amos. He is listed among the twelve so-called minor prophets of the Old Testament. He is a "minor" prophet not because he is lacking in importance, but because only remnants and fragments of his work survive. Actually, though he is designated as a prophet, he disclaimed the title himself. On one occasion Amaziah, the spiritual adviser of King Jeroboam II, attacked Amos and said, "O seer, go, flee away"—get lost. And Amos responded, "I am no prophet, nor a prophet's son." He described himself as a herdsman, a dresser of sycamore trees. That we know about him and not much else. He came from down south in Tekoa, a little village not far from Jerusalem, a place described by George Adam Smith as "without sanctity and almost without tradition." [1]

He was a blunt man, a plainspoken man. That we know about him, too, but not much else. The knowledge of his bluntness and his plainspokenness comes from a reading of the fragments that have been gathered together and are known as the book of Amos. He preached judgment.

> And he said:
> "The LORD roars from Zion,
>   and utters his voice from Jerusalem;
> the pastures of the shepherds mourn,
>   and the top of Carmel withers."

> Thus says the LORD:
> "For three transgressions of Damascus,
>   and for four, I will not revoke the punishment;
> because they have threshed Gilead
>   with threshing sledges of iron." . . .

> Thus says the LORD:
> "For three transgressions of Gaza,
>   and for four, I will not revoke the punishment;

> because they carried into exile a whole people
>   to deliver them up to Edom.
> So I will send a fire upon the wall of Gaza,
>   and it shall devour her strongholds." . . .

Thus says the LORD:
> "For three transgressions of Tyre,
>   and for four, I will not revoke the punishment;
> because they delivered up a whole people to Edom,
>   and did not remember the covenant of brotherhood." [2]

Amos did not spare anyone. He went down the whole list of nations from Damascus to Moab, and that was all right with the Israelites. However, he did not stop with foreigners.

Thus says the LORD:
> "For three transgressions of Israel,
>   and for four, I will not revoke the punishment;
> because they sell the righteous for silver,
>   and the needy for a pair of shoes—
> they that trample the head of the poor into the dust of
>   the earth,
>   and turn aside the way of the afflicted . . ." [3]

That was not all right. That was meddling at best, subversive at worst. What was more, it was meddling by an outsider. Amos came along after the twelve tribes of Israel had been divided into two nations, the ten tribes occupying the territory of northern Palestine, and little Judah clustered around the city of Jerusalem. At the time of Amos, Judah was pretty much a vassal kingdom of her larger neighbor to the north. Amos was a Judean, but he did not stay where he belonged. He went north to Bethel, straight to the sanctuary of the king of Israel, and he said there those inflammatory things about selling the righteous for silver and the needy for a pair of shoes and trampling the heads of the poor. It is bad enough to have your own kind questioning the social order, trying to change things. But when an outsider gets into the act, it is insufferable.

Furthermore, he was wrong in his predictions of doom, as any fool could plainly see. Things were going swimmingly for Israel under Jeroboam II. The gross national product was way up. Israel was prosperous, even at peace, for the most part, except for some border skirmishes that did not count. True it is, as one commentator has said: "Beneath the surface there was the mutter of discontent, but that was doubtless regarded as the transitory effect of changed conditions. Taken as a whole, the temper of the national life was confident and optimistic." [4] And into that confident, optimistic fabric of national life ripped the harsh words about judgment and national catastrophe.

> Hear this word that the LORD has spoken against you, O
> people of Israel, against the whole family which I brought
> up out of the land of Egypt:
> "You only have I known
>   of all the families of the earth;
> therefore I will punish you
>   for all your iniquities." [5]

He was not even a gentleman. Listen to his words of attack upon the well-fed matrons of Israel, words no gentleman should use to a lady.

> Hear this word, you cows of Bashan,
>   who are in the mountain of Samaria,
> who oppress the poor, who crush the needy,
>   who say to their husbands, "Bring, that we may drink!"
> The Lord GOD has sworn by his holiness
>   that, behold, the days are coming upon you,
> when they shall take you away with hooks,
>   even the last of you with fishhooks. [6]

Furthermore, he was irreverent. He refused to spare the religious institutions of his time. Bethel was a holy place. Gilgal was a shrine of some significance, apparently, and Amos vented his sarcasm on both. Listen!

> "Come to Bethel, and transgress;
>   to Gilgal, and multiply transgression;
> bring your sacrifices every morning,
>   your tithes every three days;
> offer a sacrifice of thanksgiving of that which is leavened,
>   and proclaim freewill offerings, publish them;
>   for so you love to do, O people of Israel!"
>   says the Lord GOD. [7]

> "I hate, I despise your feasts,
>   and I take no delight in your solemn assemblies.

> Even though you offer me your burnt offerings and
>   cereal offerings,
>   I will not accept them,
> and the peace offerings of your fatted beasts
>   I will not look upon.
> Take away from me the noise of your songs;
>   to the melody of your harps I will not listen.
> But let justice roll down like waters,
>   and righteousness like an everflowing stream." [8]

Tact, tolerance, discretion—none of these words could be applied to this chap Amos.

As a matter of fact, he was looked upon as a revolutionary by his contemporaries. King Jeroboam had a house preacher who slept in and took care of Jeroboam's soul, dusting off the specks on special ceremonial occasions, polishing his ego by telling him how he was an instrument of the Lord, and protecting him from hearing unpleasant things. That house preacher's name was Amaziah.

"Then Amaziah the priest of Bethel sent to Jeroboam king of Israel, saying, 'Amos has conspired against you in the midst of the house of Israel; the land is not able to bear all his words. . . .'

"And Amaziah said to Amos, 'O seer, go, flee away to the land of Judah, and eat bread there, and prophesy there; but never again prophesy at Bethel, for it is the king's sanctuary, and it is a temple of the kingdom.' " [9] Amos indignantly rejected this denunciation.

"Then Amos answered Amaziah, 'I am no prophet, nor a prophet's son; but I am a herdsman, and a dresser of sycamore trees, and the LORD took me from following the flock, and the LORD said to me, "Go, prophesy to my people Israel." ' " [10]

Of course, when he says he is not a prophet, he means he is not a professional. He did not train to be a prophet. He did not support himself by prophecy. He was a herdsman who believed he had a word from God that he must speak. That word was like a burning fire within him.

When men like that rise up outside the established church, or within it, they have a rough time. Yet, if the history of the human spirit tells us anything at all, it tells us how frequently the Holy

Spirit does work outside the traditional channels of religious institutions. This does not mean that the Holy Spirit has deserted
the church. It simply means that sometimes God has things to say
that the church does not seem to know about, or does not want
to know about.

So the Holy Spirit may speak through a poet, a journalist, a
politician, a herdsman, or a dresser of sycamore trees. There is
no telling. To decry today's injustices, today's wrongs, is never
popular, often not even safe. But it is only today's injustices that
we have a chance to change. Yet the changer usually knows pain
and rejection. Not long ago, in a newspaper article, an interview
was described with the brother of Mississippi's famed novelist
William Faulkner. In the course of the interview, the interviewer
asked the brother about his feelings regarding William Faulkner's
rejection by a large part of his native section of the country. And
in the context of that question, there were quoted some words
from Faulkner: "I love my country enough to want to cure its
faults and the only way that I can cure its faults within my ca-
pacity, within my own vocation, is to shame it, to criticize, to try
to show the difference between its evils, its good, its moments of
baseness and its moments of honesty, integrity, and pride. . . .
Just to write about the good qualities in my country wouldn't do
anything to change the bad ones. I've got to tell people about the
bad ones, so that they'd be angry enough or shamed enough to
change them." [11] There is an Amos-like attitude in that kind of
approach to responsibility.

But let us not leave Amos there scowling on the horizons of
history. There was a deep compassion in this man. His harsh
words were spoken out of concern and out of passion. The name
Amos means "burden bearer." He denounced the prosperity of
the rich because he saw the grinding poverty of the poor. He de-
cried the greed of the few because he was haunted by the pinched
faces of the many. He lamented injustice because he knew no
society could endure when injustice remained at the core of it.
The burden of the unprivileged and the underprivileged was assumed in the name of a God whose standard of measurement was
social righteousness.

"He showed me: behold, the Lord was standing beside a wall built with a plumb line, with a plumb line in his hand. And the LORD said to me, 'Amos, what do you see?' And I said, 'A plumb line.' Then the Lord said,

> 'Behold, I am setting a plumb line
>   in the midst of my people Israel;
>   I will never again pass by them;
> the high places of Isaac shall be made desolate,
>   and the sanctuaries of Israel shall be laid waste,
>   and I will rise against the house of Jeroboam with the sword.' " [12]

That plumb line against a sagging wall of national corruption. That plumb line that measured the degree of the sag, the amount of deviation from the true. Symbolic of God's standards of righteousness, held against walls built by men's hands, walls of pride and affluence and greed.

The emphasis of Amos was upon the ethical dimension of Biblical thought. That was not new, of course. It had emerged over and over again since the time of Moses. But it had been submerged by two streams of popular religion that kept erupting. On the one hand was the belief that as a covenant God, Jahweh would defend Israel come what might. He was on their side, right or wrong. And the other strand of popular belief was that the important things in religious experience were its ceremonial rites, its ritualistic sacrifices. Against both, Amos flung himself with all the power of his being; his words have burned their way into the human spirit.

> I hate, I despise your feasts,
>   and I take no delight in your solemn assemblies.
>   . . . . .
> But let justice roll down like waters,
>   and righteousness like an everflowing stream." [13]

That burden of indignation against human deprivation was one Amos would never lay down. It was born of compassion.

Nor did he lay down his vision of a God whose concern was for all people. He was the first of the great spiritual leaders of Israel who explicitly set the vision of God free from the bonds of nationalism.

"Are you not like the Ethiopians to me,
    O people of Israel?" says the LORD.
"Did I not bring up Israel from the land of Egypt,
    and the Philistines from Caphtor and the Syrians from
    Kir?" [14]

Bold comparisons, those! This rough-voiced son of the south suggests that Ethiopia, in the faraway valley of the Nile, was as precious as Israel. Did he dare compare Jahweh's leading of the Israelites, in the exodus from the land of Egypt, to his leading of the Philistines—those hereditary enemies—from Caphtor, and the Syrians from Kir? No wonder Amaziah was upset. No wonder King Jeroboam was disturbed. No wonder they both recommended to Amos that he might be happier elsewhere. Such men are menaces to domestic tranquillity.

In all probability, those words about Egypt were the last words that Amos spoke. Some later follower added that hopeful epilogue which begins with the ninth verse of the ninth chapter of Amos. Did he leave Bethel? Did he go back down south to his herds? No one really knows the time, the place, the circumstances, of his death. He fades away as all old prophets have to fade. According to one interpreter, "His is the briefest of all recorded ministries . . . his ministry did not last more than thirty minutes." [15] He made that one speech and then the king said, "Get lost," and he got lost. There is no evidence that anybody listened to him. Yet he remains a towering figure in Old Testament history, his few words living and burning, and turning Judaism in a new direction.

There is an Amos quality in all true faith. It has to be recognized and faced up to, the dark note of judgment and doom.

Maybe today is the time for it. We have lived through somber experiences in recent years. The tragic massacre of the Israelis at Munich was one of the most symbolic eruptions of our time. A world at play, celebrating the joys of physical competition, the exhilaration of games, and all the while, below the surface, violence lurked. Unresolved problems and unmitigated hatreds lay submerged, furtive and stinking and steaming. They erupted in an obscene, insane gesture of death. Play became horror and games terror-ridden, and men look at one another, made aware again of what it is to be human. And perhaps we knew again for one brief moment—as we knew when John F. Kennedy died and when Robert Kennedy died and when Martin Luther King, Jr., died and when George Wallace was struck down—the dark underside of the human spirit that keeps turning over and coming uppermost. And we knew the truth of that quotation from Aeschylus that Robert Kennedy used the night Martin Luther King, Jr., died: "In our sleep, pain which cannot forget falls drop by drop upon the heart until, in our own despair, against our will, comes wisdom through the awful grace of God." [16]

Wisdom! Does it come tortured out of reality? A wisdom that rises through pain and struggle. A wisdom that gives birth to the kind of love that takes up crosses and braces itself for agony. A wisdom, the kind of which Paul spoke, "the foolishness of God is wiser than men," [17] a grace which oftentimes cannot come until the word of judgment has been spoken.

So Amos did not have the last word. His great contemporary Hosea was far closer to this kind of wisdom. Amos had a word and it was of God. And this is a day for reminding.

> Take away from me the noise of your songs;
>   to the melody of your harps I will not listen.
> But let justice roll down like waters,
>   and righteousness like an everflowing stream. [18]

The Pain of Love

Once upon a time there was a man named Hosea. The name means "Jahweh is help." Strange name! Strange man! Strange story! A story that is difficult to untangle, difficult to place in logical sequence. Here are the beginnings of it, according to the translation of *The New English Bible:*

"The word of the Lord which came to Hosea son of Beeri during the reigns of Uzziah, Jotham, Ahaz, and Hezekiah, kings of Judah, and during the reign of Jeroboam son of Jehoash king of Israel.

"This is the beginning of the LORD's message by Hosea. He said, Go, take a wanton for your wife and get children of her wantonness; for like a wanton this land is unfaithful to the LORD. So he went and took Gomer, a worthless woman; and she conceived and bore him a son." [1]

Did Hosea know from the very beginning of his marriage that Gomer was a wanton woman? Such a view makes little sense. Actually, the whole point of the self-revelation of Hosea is that it affords an analogy of God's relationship with Israel, begun in the purity of a covenant and then, through wantonness and unfaithfulness on the part of Israel, broken and betrayed. Quite evidently, Hosea told his story from the perspective of a later point of view, in line with the theological concept of the ancient Hebrew that all things that happened were in accord with the will of God. And looking back, as he recounted his story, he saw Gomer as a loose woman from the beginning, having within her at the start the seeds of unfaithfulness. He looked back and saw her from the vantage point of the way things turned out, and he read his later insights into the very beginnings of his marriage.

The names of his children would indicate a growing awareness of the fragile nature of the relationship. The first child, born out of the joy and splendor of the early days of marriage, was called

Jezreel, "God shall sow." The second, a daughter, was Lo-ruhamah, which means "not loved, not pitied." Was there a growing rift between Gomer and Hosea? The third child was called Lo-ammi, "not my people." Was Lo-ammi thought by Hosea not even to be his own child? The analogy moves on to portray Israel and her relationship with God as such that God must say, at last, "you are not my people, and I will not be your God." [2] This intermingling of Hosea's personal tragedy with the national tragedy of his people is confusing as you read it. It is difficult at times to know whether Hosea is speaking of his home life or of the life of his people.

But the outlines are clear enough: the gradual disintegration of an intimate relationship from its pristine purity, a growing wantonness on the part of Gomer that led to her taking of lovers, a mounting indignation on the part of Hosea that led, at last, to a furious rejection.

> Is she not my wife and I her husband?
>> Plead with her to forswear those wanton looks,
>> to banish the lovers from her bosom.
>>> Or I will strip her and expose her
>>> naked as the day she was born;
>> I will make her bare as the wilderness, parched as the desert,
>>> and leave her to die of thirst.
>> I will show no love for her children;
>>> they are the offspring of wantonness,
>>> and their mother is a wanton.
>> She who conceived them is shameless;
>> she says, "I will go after my lovers;
>>> they give me my food and drink,
>> my wool and flax, my oil and my perfumes." [3]

Bitterness! Bitterness plain enough, but an amazing tenderness that even out of the rage breaks through now and then. Time passes, and Gomer's lovers grow careless of her and, at last, contemptuous. Once they had lavished gifts upon her; now it is Hosea, the discarded husband, who secretly provides.

> For she does not know that it is I who gave her
>> corn, new wine, and oil,
> I who lavished upon her silver and gold
>> which they spent on the Baal. [4]

The old rage steals back.

> I will put a stop to her merrymaking,
> her pilgrimages and new moons, her sabbaths and festivals.
>> I will punish her for the holy days
>> when she burnt sacrifices to the Baalim, when she decked
>> herself with earrings and necklaces,
> ran after her lovers and forgot me.[5]

Rage and tenderness alternate as his feelings emerge with the yearnings of Jahweh for his people of Israel. It is hard to tell when he is speaking of himself or of God. More time passes. Gomer's descent from respectable matron to prostitute is precipitous. At last, her beauty gone, her body ravaged, her face marked by dissipation, she is put up for sale, discarded and disreputable. As Edwin Lewis says: "Thereupon Hosea takes his fateful step. He will do the impossible. News has come that Gomer can be bought by anyone who is willing to pay the brothel keeper his price. The price will not be high for a woman whom few any more desire. With a word to no one, the grim-faced man sets out on his journey, and when later in the day he returns, Gomer pocked under her paint, reeking with the perfumes of her trade, slouches along by his side." [6]

He brings her back home, but as a thing purchased, not as a wife loved and accepted.

> So I got her back for fifteen pieces of silver, a homer of barley
> and a measure of wine; and I said to her,
>> Many a long day you shall live in my house
>> and not play the wanton,
> and have no intercourse with a man, nor I with you.[7]

He is still the judge, just as he sees God as the stern judge of Israel's unfaithfulness. He will not accept Gomer back, just as he believes Jahweh will not accept Israel back. She has gone too far in her wantonness, as Israel has gone too far. He will reject her as he believes Jahweh rejects Israel forever.

Thus far, his message parallels that of his harsh-voiced contemporary, Amos. Gomer has sinned, she must suffer. She has sown the wind, she must reap the whirlwind. Israel is in the same circumstances. She has been faithless; therefore, she must pay.

George Adam Smith has said of Amos: "He saw Israel from the outside. His message to her is achieved with scarcely one sob in his voice. For the sake of the poor and the oppressed among the people he is indignant. But with the erring, staggering nation as a whole he has no real sympathy." [8] So it appears with Hosea.

Then something happens. We must distinguish two Hoseas or, at least, two phases of his career. The one Hosea is the outraged, hurt, humiliated husband whose flashes of tenderness are overwhelmed by surges of indignant pride. This is the Hosea who, much like Amos, called down the wrath of God on the heads both of his erring wife and his erring country. This is the Hosea who put his wife to one side, even after he had reclaimed her, saying, "Many a long day you shall live in my house and not play the wanton . . ." How smug! How self-righteous! And how she must have hated him. Yet, he acted as the law and custom of his people required in putting aside Gomer. The adultery of a wife in Israel was looked upon sternly. Death was even the consequence under most conditions. That is why, when the prophets would denounce the unfaithfulness of Israel as a people, they used the analogy of the unfaithful wife. No more damning parallel could be conceived. To this Hosea, there was no forgiveness.

In Alan Paton's novel *Too Late the Phalarope,* the police captain in South Africa comes by night to the old Boer father to tell him how the son, a young lieutenant of police, has committed an offense against the Immorality Act and had relations with a young native girl. The old man sits in silence. At last, he calls for the Bible and opens it to the place where the family names for more than a hundred and fifty years have been recorded.

"So he took the pen and ink, and he crossed out the name of Pieter van Vlaanderen from the Book, not once but many times, not with any anger or grief that could be seen, nor with any words.

"Then he said to the captain, is there anything more? . . .

". . . he took the Book and read the words of the Hundred and Ninth Psalm, which are the most terrible words that man has ever written, and should not be in any holy book. For it is written there

"When he shall be judged, let him be condemned; and let his prayer become sin.

"Let his days be few; and let another take his office.

"Let his children be fatherless, and his wife a widow.

"Let his children be continually vagabonds, and beg; and let them seek their bread also out of their desolate places.

"Let the extortioner catch all that he hath; and let the strangers spoil his labour.

"Let there be none to extend mercy unto him; neither let there be any to favour his fatherless children.

"Let his posterity be cut off; and in the generation following let their name be blotted out. . . .

". . . he said in a voice of agony, I shall not pray. . . . He stayed there for a minute maybe, till he had mastered himself; then he raised his head and closed the Book; and stood up from his chair, turning away from us, and making for the stairs to his room." [9]

It was the police captain who later said, "if man takes unto himself God's right to punish, then he must also take upon himself God's promise to restore." [10]

When did that fact break upon the man Hosea? If a man takes upon himself God's right to punish, then he must also take upon himself God's right to restore. How did it come about? The first Hosea was a Hosea of condemnation, the other Hosea a Hosea of restoration and of hope. How did it happen? Did he find his love for Gomer so real that, at last, it embraced and enshrouded all the hurt and the humiliation? Did he break through to a new vision of God, and did that say something to him about this beaten, broken woman? Did a startling message come through to him that Jahweh loves Israel so that he cannot cast her aside? How then can a man cast someone aside? Did his experience of abiding love for a woman open his heart to the limitless love of God for his people? Or did the two experiences, the one with God and the one with Gomer, so intermingle and intertwine that they could not and cannot be separated? He knew only that love is final. It must have the last word—the love of God, the love of man.

However it came to him, it overwhelmed his message of judgment and swallowed up the notes of retribution.

He says: "I will woo her, I will go with her into the wilderness and comfort her . . ." [11] And that phrase "comfort her" can be translated more literally, "I will speak home to her heart." "On that day she shall call me 'My husband' and shall no more call me 'My Baal' . . ." [12] George Adam Smith says: ". . . to an Israelite some of these terms must have brought back the days of his wooing. *I will speak home to her heart* is a forcible expression, like . . . the sweet Scottish 'it cam' up roond my heart,' and was used in Israel as from man to woman when he won her." [13]

Hosea does not say he is weeping but you hear the sounds of wrenching sobs. His sentences are short and sharp, contrasted with the measured form of Amos' denunciatory sentences. The bulk of the book of Hosea is literal poetry as this other Hosea bursts into singing. Everywhere he sees the redemptive power of love. He changes his figure from that of husband and wife to that of father and son. He says, in the name of God:

When Israel was a child, I loved him,
    and out of Egypt I called my son.
The more I called them,
    the more they went from me;
they kept sacrificing to the Baals,
    and burning incense to idols.
Yet it was I who taught Ephraim to walk,
    I took them up in my arms;
    but they did not know that I healed them.
I led them with cords of compassion,
    with the bands of love,
and I became to them as one
    who eases the yoke on their jaws,
    and I bent down to them and fed them. [14]

Again he asks in the name of God:

How can I give you up, O Ephraim!
    How can I hand you over, O Israel!
How can I make you like Admah!
    How can I treat you like Zeboiim!

My heart recoils within me,
my compassion grows warm and tender.

....

for I am God and not man,
the Holy One in your midst,
and I will not come to destroy.[15]

Hosea never loses sight of the awfulness of the apostasy his people. He is no less realistic than Amos at that point. But the point at which he goes beyond Amos is in the sensing of the greater awfulness of God's love, awful in the original sense of that word, awe-inspiring, overwhelming in majesty. It is a love that will not give up, will not let go. It is a love that is dogged and determined. It is a love that is steadfast even when tear-drenched. It is a love that a psalmist once glimpsed and cried out, "If I ascend to heaven, thou art there! If I make my bed in Sheol, thou art there!"[16]

In his vision of that love, a love wrenched out of personal agony, Hosea went beyond Amos toward the daring thought that, above all else and beyond all else, God is love. That is the first time it comes through clearly in the tradition of the Old Testament.

And emerging from Hosea's words, we begin to see the outline of a cross. From his words? No, not just from his words but from his life, from his own experience of brokenness to the wholeness of love. You see him stumbling through the black night in rage, indignation, and hate, in a struggle for the ability to forgive. This does not come cheap. And out of his own struggle comes a realization of the forgiveness of God, which does not come cheap, either. He staggered, bleeding, into the presence of God to find that what he had learned of the mystery of human love was the secret of God, too. He came to know that pain of involvement in someone else's shame that enabled him to grasp life's final meaning, which is to know God. To be a lover is to expose oneself to rejection and to betrayal.

Once upon a time there was a man named Hosea, or two of him really. One is the stern voice of judgment. And then, the other Hosea comes striding out of the shadows, holding his heart in his hand and saying, "See! See! See what God is like!" And all of it—the hurt and the humiliation, the rage and the throbbing pain—began to make a little sense as they were gathered up into the arms of a God who said:

> I will heal their faithlessness;
>> I will love them freely,
>> for my anger has turned from them.
> I will be as the dew to Israel;
>> he shall blossom as the lily,
>> he shall strike root as the poplar;
> his shoots shall spread out;
>> his beauty shall be like the olive,
>> and his fragrance like Lebanon.
> They shall return and dwell beneath my shadow,

> their fragrance shall be like the wine of Lebanon.[17]

The Sleep of the Innocent

Once upon a time there was a man named Jonah, so the story goes, and the word of the Lord came to Jonah, saying: " 'Go to the great city of Nineveh, go now and denounce it, for its wickedness stares me in the face.' But Jonah set out for Tarshish to escape from the LORD. He went down to Joppa, where he found a ship bound for Tarshish. He paid his fare and went on board, meaning to travel by it to Tarshish out of reach of the LORD." [1]

The word of the Lord came to Jonah, and he took a slow boat to Tarshish to get away from the word of the Lord. But it did not work. The storyteller affirms: ". . . the LORD let loose a hurricane, and the sea ran so high in the storm that the ship threatened to break up." [2] Jonah was down below deck, sleeping the sleep of the innocent, I suppose, secure in his feeling that by the time he got home from this expedition to Tarshish, God would have forgotten about Nineveh. Jonah did not approve of the Ninevites, he did not like the Ninevites. He had a supreme confidence in the power of his own preaching, and he was afraid that if he preached repentance to the Ninevites, they would repent, and God would have mercy on them, and the city would be saved from its just fate. Jonah wanted Nineveh destroyed. He did not like the Ninevites, he did not approve of them.

So he was down below, waiting for God to come round to his way of seeing things. The frightened ship captain broke in upon his slumbers. He demanded that Jonah get to prayer to whatever God he might believe in. Then, touching all bases, the sailors cast lots to see who was to blame for their bad luck. The blackball fell on the man called Jonah.

The sailors were not mean men. They continued to try to fight the storm. They were not cruel men, just frightened men. The thing about frightened men is they can do cruel things. They did it. They decided, at last, to throw Jonah into the sea. They

101

did it with a prayer, as such things are often done, and they did
it with a pious affirmation that it was the "will" of God. They
could not help it and, therefore, were not responsible, as such
things are often explained. For, the storyteller tells us: "At last
they called on the LORD and said, 'O LORD, do not let us perish
at the price of this man's life; do not charge us with the death
of an innocent man. All this, O LORD, is thy set purpose.' " ³

It was predestined. They took Jonah and threw him over-
board. That is where the story of Jonah becomes a fish story.
That is the only part of it that most people even remember. Great
arguments have arisen now and again on the feasibility, or the
lack of feasibility, of a man's spending three days and three nights
in the belly of a whale. I remember reading about one chap who
went to great trouble, measuring the inner dimensions of a whale
to prove that Jonah could have sat up, lain down, and even moved
about a bit. Jonah, according to the story, lived in that whale.

And Jonah prayed as any man in similar circumstances would
have prayed, and he made great promises, as any man in similar
circumstances would have done, too. "Then the LORD spoke to
the fish and it spewed Jonah out on to the dry land. The word
of the LORD came to Jonah a second time . . ." ⁴

The second time around, Jonah did not argue. He may have
mumbled a bit under his breath, but he obeyed. "Jonah obeyed
at once and went to Nineveh. He began by going a day's journey
into the city, a vast city, three days' journey across . . ." ⁵ And
he preached a message of repentance, and things turned out just
as he had feared they would. "When the news reached the king
of Nineveh he rose from his throne, stripped off his robes of state,
put on sackcloth and sat in ashes." ⁶

It was about as successful a preaching mission as any traveling
evangelist could hope for. "God saw what they did, and how they
abandoned their wicked ways, and he repented and did not bring
upon them the disaster he had threatened." ⁷

If the story ended here, it would be a delightful tale of a mission accomplished. But it does not end here. For the story really
is not about Nineveh, it is about Jonah. And listen to Jonah:
"Jonah was greatly displeased and angry, and he prayed to the

LORD: 'This, O LORD, is what I feared when I was in my own country, and to forestall it I tried to escape to Tarshish; I knew that thou art "a god gracious and compassionate, long-suffering and ever constant, and always willing to repent of the disaster." And now, LORD, take my life: I should be better dead than alive.' " [8]

How can men possibly surround this delicious satire with solemn claptrap about the dimensions of a whale? This is a parable of human pretense and prejudice. It is a comedy of punctured pride, a tragedy of narrow vision. It was written in a time of growing intolerance on the part of the Jews toward other races and peoples, written as a satire on that intolerance, as a ridiculous caricature of the self-righteous and the separatist. It is a mixture of human pettiness set over against the magnitude of the grace of God. We laugh at Jonah lest we cry for what he reveals to us of ourselves. Irreverent? Jonah was made to be laughed at. As Carl Knopf puts it: "The author respects no dignity. Jonah is made ludicrous—trying to get away from God: quoting current theology about a merciful, forgiving, loving God while hoping it is not true; bothered about a gourd vine while oblivious to the fate of a nation; losing his temper and acting childish when he cannot have his own way." [9]

Jonah came face to face with God and learned that what he had professed to know all along about God and the love of God was true. He learned God meant it. He learned that the world was bigger than he thought it was. He had thought it was no bigger than his own people, Israel; no larger than his kind of folk. He thought that where he lived was the very center of the universe. He knew about Nineveh, by hearsay, and what he knew was not good. Therefore, when he heard of the threatened downfall of the wicked city, he could not care less. If Jonah's concern was not big enough to embrace the city of Nineveh, how could God's concern be? That is a common enough attitude. We all decide who are the elect and the non-elect. Is not God like us? Does he not understand as we understand? Does he not bring to bear upon life and people the same values? Is he not as appreciative as we are of who counts? Of course, he is.

Jonah found out that an identification of his narrow concerns and his little loves with the great big heart of God was presumptuous. He found out that an identification of his dislikes and his prejudices with the attitudes of God was bumptious arrogance. Judaism had always had its strain of universalism even before the writing of the book of Jonah. In the Midrash there is a tale of how the ministering angels around the throne of God in heaven burst into song at the overthrow of the Egyptian army in the Red Sea at the time of the Exodus. And a voice thundered out from the throne: "My children lie drowned in the sea, and you would sing?" Jonah had to learn that the God of Abraham, Isaac, and Jacob had an eye out for Nineveh, too, that wicked city. The world was bigger and God was bigger than Jonah had ever thought. Jonah had acted upon the assumption that the world was no bigger than Israel and God was confined to the territorial limitations of Palestine. Jonah was wrong!

Jonah came face to face with God and found that we cannot stereotype people when we come face to face with the God who made people. We cannot bundle them all up into one great package and have done with them. We cannot wad them together in groups and label them and then forget them. Just as we cannot catalog God as though he were a biological specimen, so we cannot catalog his children and pin them into place. We cannot stereotype them by color or race or religion, or by goodness or badness, or in any other way.

The wise and gentle British theologian H. H. Farmer, of Cambridge, warned a group of parsons against the development of a narrow professional interest in people, seeing them as "souls" to be "saved," as persons to be changed. Then he told of his colleague, Carnegie Simpson, whose maid had won five thousand pounds in the Irish Sweepstakes. She kept nothing of the money that she had won. She set up a home for her aged father, put her brother in business, and paid the hospital bills of an unemployed sister. And Simpson confessed that he felt that she, unattended by the ministrations of the clergy, should have gone straight to the dogs.

And then, Farmer went on to tell one of his own experiences

on a train, as he was seated in a smoking car next to a group of men who were gambling for rather high stakes—gambling and talking about their homes, their children, and their gardens. He confessed, "I felt, to my horror, a faint feeling of disappointment flit across my mind. I felt as a professional that men who gambled so enthusiastically should not have so profound a feeling for the decent things of life." They broke his stereotypes, you see. We all have that tendency to stereotype and to limit God's grace to the regular channels, particularly to those that we can control. In Jonah's mind, Ninevites were Ninevites. What business had they repenting and being recipients of the mercies of God?

Jonah was a good man, a professional good man. He was a prophet. There was probably not a vicious bone in his body. He was one of those people whom Dr. Harry Overstreet has labeled the "gentle people of prejudice" that we always have with us. Courteous, kindly, well-meaning, gentle people. They know what is best and who is best, and they know exactly where God stands on all things.

Jonah came face to face with God, and it changed his whole view of the world. It even threatened to change his religion, and that was not easy. It took that hurricane to start the process of change, and it was only on the second time around, remember, that he obeyed the word of the Lord and went to Nineveh. And, as he feared, the Ninevites repented. And, as he feared, God forgave them. And there he was, good orthodox Jew that he was, with all those outsiders bleating about his God and claiming to know what the love of God meant.

The last we see of him he is sitting under that gourd vine, that castor-oil plant, sulking, sulking. The last words we hear from him are: "I should be better dead than alive," and God asking, "Are you so angry?" "Yes, mortally angry." That is what he said. The last we hear from Jonah's God are these words: "You are sorry for the gourd, though you did not have the trouble of growing it, a plant which came up in a night and withered in a night. And should not I be sorry for the great city of Nineveh, with its hundred and twenty thousand who cannot tell their right hand from their left, and cattle without number?" [10]

And then, no answer from Jonah. The whole structure of the way things are was shaking for him. What happened to him? Maybe he just stayed there sulking. Maybe he poisoned himself on hate. I do not know. Maybe the story ends the way it does because it is a tale not over. It is still being acted out.

Do you see yourself at all in the story of Jonah? Or the church in the story of Jonah? Or the nation in the story of Jonah? Or white Americans in the story of Jonah? The church was founded on faith in the one who said, "Go into all the world." Yet we spend time tidying up the front yard because we do not even want to go around the block. And if something goes the way we do not like, we sulk, mortally angry.

The final thing is a kind of wandering, is it not? Jonah found out that the world was far bigger than he thought, but not big enough to escape from God—not even in Tarshish, which was on the farthest side of Spain, the very edge of the known world.

Each of us, finally, makes his own response. Each of us is Jonah to some extent, of course. The word of the Lord came to Jonah and Jonah went down to Joppa. He took ship to Tarshish to escape the word of the Lord. He did not make it. Poor Jonah! He tried to get away from the grace of God, to get outside its limits, and that cannot be done.

The Frailty of a Blameless Man

Once upon a time there was a man named Job. He is a proverbial figure. To speak of the "sufferings of Job" conjures up an image of unbearable sorrows and catastrophic blows. We refer to someone who endures the incredible as having the "patience of Job," though actually as we read his story in the Old Testament, he was a fanatically impatient man, not at all static or resigned. There is even a colloquialism by which we describe those who live in utter poverty as being "as poor as Job's turkey."

Once upon a time there was a man named Job, and thereby hangs a tale. A wild tale of disaster piled upon disaster. A throbbing tale of sobbing in the night and lamentation at high noon. A shining tale of a search for answers to the age-old question: Why do the innocent suffer? A dark tale enacted under a leaden sky.

Job's story is one of horror, his saga is swathed in pain. It begins: "There lived in the land of Uz a man of blameless and upright life named Job, who feared God and set his face against wrongdoing. He had seven sons and three daughters; and he owned seven thousand sheep and three thousand camels, five hundred yoke of oxen and five hundred asses, with a large number of slaves. Thus Job was the greatest man in all the East." [1]

The lightning flashed and the sheep died. The Chaldaeans came and the camels were driven off. The Sabaeans swooped down, and the oxen and the asses were taken, the herdsmen slain. And the whirlwind descended and struck a house, and the seven sons and three daughters died. "At this Job stood up and rent his cloak; then he shaved his head and fell prostrate on the ground, saying:

> Naked I came from the womb,
> naked I shall return whence I came.
> The LORD gives and the LORD takes away;
> blessed be the name of the LORD.

Throughout all this Job did not sin; he did not charge God with unreason." [2]

Not yet! But his agony was not done. Job was smitten with running sores from head to foot, so that he took a piece of broken pot to scratch himself as he sat among the ashes.

What a man! Let us take a look at him. Let us walk around him. Let us hear what we can hear, see what we can see. The man called Job, for example, was a raiser of questions. Listen to him!

> Why should the sufferer be born to see the light?
> Why is life given to men who find it so bitter?
> . . . . .
> Why should a man be born to wander blindly,
> hedged in by God on every side?
> . . . . .
> Have I the strength to wait?
> What end have I to expect, that I should be patient?
> Is my strength the strength of stone?
> or is my flesh bronze?
> Oh how shall I find help within myself?
> The power to aid myself is put out of my reach.
> . . . . .
> What is man that thou makest much of him
> and turnest thy thoughts towards him,
> only to punish him morning by morning
> or to test him every hour of the day?
> Wilt thou not look away from me for an instant?
> Wilt thou not let me be while I swallow my spittle?
> . . . . .
> Why didst thou bring me out of the womb?
> . . . . .
> Why do the wicked enjoy long life,
> hale in old age, and great and powerful?
> . . . . .
> What is the Almighty that we should worship him,
> or what should we gain by seeking his favour? [3]

Those are questions for you, questions that go deep into the human heart and thrust high into the heavens. Questions hard as stone, flung against the rigid orthodoxy of his day. Questions that demand answers. Questions never before asked, at least not in the Biblical record. Questions aimed at the belief of the Hebrews in a direct relationship between human conduct and human suffering. Whoever wrote the book of Job (and in all probability it was the product of a school of storytellers over a period of time) was questioning the hitherto unquestioned, such as the assumption that if one suffered it was because one had sinned. This was questioned by the very opening of the drama. "There lived in the land of Uz a man of blameless and upright life named Job, who feared God and set his face against wrongdoing." [4] To such a man as that came calamity after calamity.

The old orthodoxy was questioned by having Job lash back at Bildad the Shuhite, who moaned that man is a maggot and a worm, totally unclean before God. Job said to him:

> I swear by God, who has denied me justice,
> and by the Almighty, who has filled me with bitterness:
> so long as there is any life left in me
> and God's breath is in my nostrils,
> no untrue word shall pass my lips
> and my tongue shall utter no falsehood.
> God forbid that I should allow you to be right;
> till death, I will not abandon my claim to innocence.
> I will maintain the rightness of my cause, I will never give up;
> so long as I live, I will not change.[5]

That is what Job said.

The old orthodoxy was questioned by having Job's questions spilling out all over everywhere, but never a direct answer was given to them, as though they were unanswerable. It was questioned by having Job reject all the platitudes of his friends and stand alone, at last, under the unyielding sky. It was questioned centuries later when Jesus of Nazareth followed up the questions, saying: "Your Father . . . sends rain on the just and on the unjust"; saying to his disciples: "In the world you will have trouble"; saying: "If any man would come after me . . . let him . . . take up his cross . . ." "And then," as Clark Hunt says, "as though words were not enough, there was a cross on a hill one Friday afternoon to further confound the descendants of Job's friends who had reduced God to a pair of scales." [6]

Job was an accuser, an angry man, indignant and blunt. Listen to him!

After this Job broke silence and cursed the day of his birth:
Perish the day when I was born
and the night which said, 'A man is conceived'!
May that day turn to darkness; may God above not look for it,
nor light of dawn shine on it.
May blackness sully it, and murk and gloom,
cloud smother that day, swift darkness eclipse its sun.
Blind darkness swallow up that night;
count it not among the days of the year,
reckon it not in the cycle of the months.
That night, may it be barren for ever,
no cry of joy be heard in it.

There is no peace of mind nor quiet for me;
I chafe in torment and have no rest.

But I will not hold my peace;
I will speak out in the distress of my mind
and complain in the bitterness of my soul.

I am in despair, I would not go on living;
leave me alone, for my life is but a vapour.

I am sickened of life;
I will give free rein to my griefs,
I will speak out in bitterness of soul.
I will say to God, 'Do not condemn me,
but tell me the ground of thy complaint against me.'

Man born of woman is short-lived and full of disquiet.
He blossoms like a flower and then he withers;
he slips away like a shadow and does not stay;
he is like a wine-skin that perishes
or a garment that moths have eaten.

If I cry 'Murder!' no one answers;
if I appeal for help, I get no justice.
He has walled in my path so that I cannot break away ... [7]

Honest and plain, this man Job, outspoken and daring. Archibald MacLeish has one of his characters in *J.B.* refer to "a desperate stubbornness / Fighting the inextinguishable stars." [8] That is Job! Saying the things most men feel at one time or another, cutting through all the glittering generalities his friends were spin-ning to hold him in the fantasyland in which they lived.

Once in a seminar in 1931, the theologian Karl Barth heard one of his students make a remark that, according to Luther, the curses of the damned sometimes are more acceptable to God than the hallelujahs of the pious. That student was Dietrich Bonhoeffer. What did Bonhoeffer and Martin Luther mean? They meant that sometimes the damned take God more seriously than the shallow and facile righteous. Sometimes God matters more to a man in the torments of hell, wrestling with despair, crying out his rebellion, than he does to the man who minces daintily around the fringes of the faith, holding back from burning feelings either of deep doubt or of passionate belief. Job, in his accusations, was closer to God than his friends in their unthinking orthodoxy.

Job was a proud man, a man of integrity. The whole thirty-first chapter of the book of Job is given over to a defense by Job of the record of his life, and he concludes:

> Let me but call a witness in my defence!
> Let the Almighty state his case against me!
> . . . . .
> I would plead the whole record of my life
> and present that in court as my defence.

Then:

> Job's speeches are finished.[9]

It is amazing that God is never presented as reproving the pride of Job. Richard B. Sewall says: ". . . the Poem as a whole makes an important statement about pride, which the Greeks were to make repeatedly, though from a different perspective. According to the Poet, and to the Greek tragedians, pride like Job's is justified. It has its ugly and dark side, but it was through pride that Job made his spiritual gains and got a hearing from Jehovah himself. The Lord favored Job's pride and rebuked the safe orthodoxy of the Counselors. The pride that moved Job is the dynamic of a whole line of tragic heroes, from Oedipus to [Herman Melville's] Ahab." [10]

Job was a lonely man. Novelist Thomas Wolfe, who knew what loneliness meant, wrote: "The most tragic, sublime, and beautiful expression of human loneliness which I have ever read is the Book of Job." [11] Job had a wife, but she was not much help, at least as far as the record goes. "Then his wife said to him, 'Are you still unshaken in your integrity? Curse God and die!' But he answered, 'You talk as any wicked fool of a woman might talk. If we accept good from God, shall we not accept evil?' " [12]

"Job appears in Mohammedan legend; he swears to give his wife a hundred stripes when he gets well, but Allah tells him to let her off with one blow from a hundred-leave palm branch." [13] Allah was aware that Job's wife played a hard role. She does deserve a good word. After all, they were *her* children, too. She probably had her difficulties to endure without even friends to console her. Being married to a man in trouble is not easy.

She did not understand him, apparently, nor did he understand her. Her loneliness, in part, was his fault. But then, he had three friends. "When Job's three friends, Eliphaz of Teman, Bildad of Shuah, and Zophar of Naamah, heard of all these calamities which had overtaken him, they left their homes and arranged to come and condole with him and comfort him. But when they first saw him from a distance, they did not recognize him; and they wept aloud, rent their cloaks and tossed dust into the air over their heads." Then they had good sense—they kept quiet. "For seven days and seven nights they sat beside him on the ground, and none of them said a word to him; for they saw that his suffering was very great." [14]

They came running when they heard what had happened. They probably came running out of mixed motives, as most of us do. I am sure that when they heard of Job's troubles, they dropped everything, saying to one another, "Now is the time to rally round good old Job." Their concern was sincere. But then, too, being human, there were less worthy, probably unconscious, motives. They wanted to do some evangelistic work on the basis of their pet theories. They wanted to convince Job of the depth of their own insights. Each of them had his own approach, his own emphasis.

MacLeish puts them in modern garb in *J.B.* One of them is

a communist who has a political answer, another one is a clergy-man who has a churchly answer, and the third is a psychiatrist who has a psychiatrist's answer. Each of them had his own party line. They all agreed on one thing—they all agreed on pointing the finger at the man on the ash heap and in urging him to con-fess his sins. If Job was defiantly proud, they were insufferably smug.

Once Alexander Pope said: "I never knew any man in my life who could not bear another's misfortunes perfectly like a Christian." [15] That spirit marked the friends of Job. Their names are interesting. One of them was Eliphaz, which "probably means 'God crushes,' Bildad is short for 'Darling of God,' and Zophar may be rendered in three playful ways, 'Twittering Bird,' 'Jumping Goat,' or 'Sharp Nail.' " [16] Quite a trio! Three friends, but Job was lonely.

Once upon a time there was a proud, lonely, obstinate man called Job, a question-raiser. At the beginning, he raises his ques-tion: Why do the innocent suffer? It is never answered. As he moves toward the experience of the mystery, and as he moves into the experience of the meaning beyond the mystery, that ques-tion loses its urgency. It loses its urgency because it is never answered. There is no reason to keep asking it. Probably be-cause it cannot be answered. When all the words are ended, God answers Job and his friends out of the whirlwind, saying:

> Who is this whose ignorant words
> cloud my design in darkness?
> Brace yourself and stand up like a man;
> I will ask questions, and you shall answer.[17]

Then, to God's words at the very end, Job once more speaks:

> I had heard of thee by the hearing of the ear,
>   but now my eye sees thee . . .[18]

And it is done. There is no answer, no vindication of Job's own integrity, no vindication of God's purposes; only the final mys-tery, and the experiencing of meaning and mystery.

So the man called Job was God's man at last, drawn back out

of his isolation and his alienation into life. That is what it is all about.

Once upon a time? Mr. Zuss says carelessly:

> Oh, there's always
> Someone playing Job.

And Mr. Nickles replies broodingly:

> Job is everywhere we go,
>   His children dead, his work for nothing,
> Counting his losses, scraping his boils,
> Discussing himself with his friends and physicians,
> Questioning everything—the times, the stars,
> His own soul, God's providence.[19]

There is always someone playing Job. And each of us has a Job-like role of his own at some time or other (or at least we deem it so)—an hour when our confidence in goodness is blasted, a moment when the world at large goes crazy and our own little private worlds are shaking, a day when we are driven out into the storm, and the wind clutches at our clothing and the rain drives full in our face.

Once upon a time? No, not once upon a time. "There's always someone playing Job." Thus Job points us toward the suffering of Jesus, which is dramatized during Lent. The mystery of suffering is heightened by the cross on Golgotha and by Jesus' faith on that dark Friday. Is that why Jesus means so much? Job would have understood Jesus. He would have understood what he said about God and about unconquerable faith and his love. He would have heard those words from the cross "My God, my God, why hast thou forsaken me?" and he would have understood. Job would have comprehended the cross. For that lonely, obstinate, accusing man Job was God's man at last. And his ash heap, in the Old Testament, is very close to that cross in the New Testament. For the cross even represents God himself playing Job, involved in all our frailty and hurts and hopes, understanding us.

EPILOGUE

Our stories are all told. The tales of human frailty and divine gentleness are complete—or are they? Are not these ancient stories out of the past as contemporary as the morning newspaper? Is that not why the Bible is still a living Word from God? For the Bible is not an abstract treatise concerning the nature of God. It is not a philosophical discussion of his nature and attributes. It is instead a concrete recitation of events, of God's part in these events, and of human reactions to the events and to the God who revealed himself in them. The difference between the Biblical approach to religious reality and our usual approach is significant. We begin with abstractions. The Bible is always concrete. We carry forward our interpretations of reality by argument and discussion. The Bible begins in someone's life. The Bible always moves from someone's confrontation with God to an understanding of that confrontation. We are given to the effort to move from the understanding back to the confrontation. It cannot be done.

We cannot understand Paul, for example, by beginning at his involved, somewhat convoluted arguments concerning God's relationship to the Jews as Paul sets it forth in the Letter to the Romans. If we want to understand Paul we must go to his story as it is told three times in the book of Acts,[1] twice in words attributed to Paul himself. There you catch the deep-rooted nature of his Jewishness. There you see the complete transformation from his early manner of life to the manner that marked his Christian experience and his mission to the Gentiles. Add to the conversion accounts Paul's words to the Philippians in which he describes himself as "a Hebrew born of Hebrews."[2]

The story is always what matters. The story of Creation is a tale of a grace-filled world into which intruded the angular distortion of human pride and frailty. The story ever since is fraught with the repetition of the evidences of both human frailty and the gentle grace of God. From the frailty have come the estrangement of man and his brother, the betrayal of love by lust, the brutality of aggression, the fear-filled abandonment of integrity and honor. From the frailty have come the frantic efforts to escape God and to escape one another and to escape ourselves. From the grace have come the tender trembling of hope, the shaking ecstacy of love, and the shivering excitement of faith. We human beings limp along awkwardly and helplessly, our emotions twisted and our lives wrenched out of shape. We live without grace and often without gentleness, the contours of our lives formless and irregular. We bump into one another and the sharp edges of our feelings cut and lacerate. We are sorry at times for what we do to each other, even sorrier for ourselves and for what others do to us. But we are confused and puzzled by our graceless living, knowing life should not be this way. So we strive and strain for a time, make good resolutions and reach out tentatively toward someone we have hurt. We gird up our moral loins and determine we will be different, more outgoing and open, more honest and reliable. Then the whole business collapses and we are back where we were, morally flaccid, spiritually inert, and emotionally depressed. We are in dis-grace, out of favor, if not with others, at least with ourselves. We have wrestled like Jacob with a stranger and come off crippled and beaten. We have fled like Jonah from a task that has become disagreeable. Because our lives are awry, the whole world seems awry.

Then comes the time to stop and wait and recoup. For grace is not grasped or seized by human initiative. If the stories in this book convey truth, life is wound "round and round / as if with air" by grace. The world and life are not always graceful but both the world and life are grace-filled. God created this world and saw that it was good. He created man and looked upon his creation and saw that it was very good. He came after Adam and Eve, frightened and in hiding, calling to them by name. He placed on the murderer Cain the mark of his watch-care. He remembered Noah amid the wild emptiness of the flood. He gave a new name to Jacob at his time of self-recognition. He turned

Sarah's laughter of derision into the laughter of joy that a son was born. He took David's passionate spirit and set it to music. All through the Bible we find man on the run and God on the roam, turning up anywhere and everywhere, from the king's palace to the shepherd's hut. That is the way it still is—man on the run, trying desperately to get away; God on the roam, refusing to abandon his fleeing sons and daughters. That is why we must stop and wait at times, look around us and see how we are surrounded. We are hemmed in, and all the flailing in the world will not get us free of grace. "There is nothing but God's grace," wrote Robert Louis Stevenson in *The Ebb Tide*. "We walk upon it, we breathe it; we live and die by it; it makes the nails and axles of the universe . . ."

That is what the stories in this book are all about. That is what the Christian faith is all about. That is what you and I are all about at the heart of us. And that is why the story of human frailty and divine grace is your story and my story. Your story may take a vastly different direction from mine, but the same essential ingredients are present in both of them. It is that way with the stories in this book. The experience of Adam was not that of Cain, nor was the experience of Jacob that of Moses. Abraham was a far different person from his grandson Isaac. Saul and David were two completely different kinds of king. Yet through all of these varied and multicolored lives there ran human need and divine help. Not all of them responded, but the divine help was there. That is what their stories illustrate as surely as they illustrate the presence of sin and frailty. God never let any of them go.

Perhaps these people from the past will help you understand your story. Perhaps their stories will help you get perspective on yourself. For their basic frailties—anxiety, lust, greed, superstitious fear, self-righteousness, cruelty—are perennial. Our problem in handling them is perennial too. Even church members who stand tall in their places on Sunday and affirm the creed are not always sure of who they are when their frailties toss them into guilty panic. In more than a quarter of a century of pastoral work I have been struck by the inability of Christians to deal with their humanness, in either its strengths or its weaknesses. Unassuaged guilt is a dark shadow in the lives of people who cannot accept the incorrigible nature of God's love. So they laugh too loudly and play too hard or drink too much; they punish themselves in all sorts of indirect ways; they work too hard and drive themselves without mercy. And still the angel stands east of Eden with his flaming sword, and we remain outside, all of us. For the story of Adam and Eve is the story of every human being. That is why this ancient legend has endured through the centuries. And Eden tempts us, Eden as the place of innocence. We want to go back. But we cannot. When God asked the man, "Did you eat of the fruit of the tree?" he answered yes. But then he added, "But I am blameless, for the woman gave it to me." God asked the woman, "Did you eat of the fruit of the tree?" "Yes," she replied, and added: "But I am blameless. The serpent seduced me." Here at the beginning of the human story is the everlasting temptation to return to innocence, to the feeling that we are without blame.

But there is no return. Paul is right, as dark as his words seem: "None is righteous, no, not one." [3] Innocence cannot be regained. A newspaper story of the conversion of famed playwright Tennessee Williams to the Roman Catholic church after a near-fatal bout with influenza attributed to Mr. Williams the statement of his need: "I want my goodness back again." This lament for a lost innocence is plaintive but naïve. The church cannot give us back our innocence. Nothing and no one can. We accept our involvement in the human family and we look upon our nakedness.

What then? Must we despair? No! The whole point of the gospel is that we must not despair in our frailty, for it is as we are that God calls us. His grace is offered not to blameless ones, not to innocents dwelling in some mythical garden of Eden, but to men and women as they are, the kind of men and women with whom Christ identified himself. One of the profoundest insights of Dietrich Bonhoeffer is found in a letter written in July of 1944, after more than a year of imprisonment. He wrote, "I discovered and am still discovering up to this very moment that it is only by living completely in this world that one learns to believe. One must abandon every attempt to make something of oneself, whether it be a saint, a converted sinner, a churchman . . . a righteous man or an unrighteous one, a sick man or a healthy one. That is what I mean by wordliness—taking life in one's stride, with all its duties and problems, its successes and failures, its experiences and helplessness. It is in such a life that we throw ourselves utterly in the arms of God . . ." [4] Reread the Biblical stories of Adam and Eve, of Abraham and David, and all the rest of them. Not an innocent in the lot! But not one whose life was not wound with grace and touched by God's gentleness.

When we turn to the New Testament we find that the songs those early Christians sang are not laments for lost innocence. They are triumph songs of the grace of God. They are songs of forgiveness and of acceptance and renewal. Paul called himself a wretched man when he faced his inner conflicts and asked: "Who will deliver me from this body of death?" Then the answer follows hard upon the question: "Thanks be to God through Jesus Christ our Lord!" [5] Here, then, is no lament for a lost innocence but a great shout. No moaning but a great laughter. No sobbing but a tremendous joy. No whining but a sound of singing. No looking back but a looking ahead. For the direction of the gospel is not a return to a lost Eden but an adventure in movement toward a new Jerusalem. There is no belittling of our humanness but a rejoicing in our human potential. Not "I want my goodness back," but "Thanks be to God, who gives us the victory through our Lord Jesus Christ." [6] From frailty through grace to abundant living!

NOTES

All Scripture is from the Revised Standard Version unless otherwise noted.

Introduction

1. Malcolm Cowley, "Storytelling's Tarnished Image," *Saturday Review*, Sept. 25, 1971, p. 25.
2. Elie Wiesel, *The Gates of the Forest* (New York: Avon Books, 1967).
3. T. S. Eliot, *Ash Wednesday* (New York: Harcourt Brace Jovanovich, 1930), p. 19.
4. Gerard Manley Hopkins, "Mary Mother of Divine Grace," in *Poems and Prose of Gerard Manley Hopkins* (London: Penguin Books, 1958), p. 55.

A Tale of Peril and Promise

1. Quoted in Will and Ariel Durant, *The Age of Louis XIV* (New York: Simon and Schuster, 1963), p. 493.
2. Gen. 1:1-2, 26-27.
3. Gen. 1:27.
4. Gen. 2:7.
5. Gen. 1:27, 31.
6. William Hazlitt, quoted in Roger Lincoln Shinn, *Life, Death, and Destiny* (Philadelphia: The Westminster Press, 1957), p. 21.
7. Gen. 2:21-24.
8. Gen. 2:25.
9. Gen. 2:15-17.
10. Gen. 3:1-6.
11. Gen. 3:7.
12. Gen. 3:8-13.
13. Gen. 3:23-24.
14. Gen. 3:7.
15. Gen. 3:8-9.

Sins Too Big for God?

1. From *East of Eden* by John Steinbeck. Copyrighted 1952 by John Steinbeck. Reprinted by permission of The Viking Press, Inc.
2. Gen. 4:1-5, 8.

3. *The Interpreter's Bible* (Nashville: Abingdon Press, 1952), Vol. I, pp. 516-517.
4. Gen. 4:9-10.
5. Gen. 4:17.
6. Albert Camus, *The Stranger* (New York: Alfred A. Knopf, 1946), p. 1.
7. Quoted in Jean-Paul Sartre, "An Explication of *The Stranger,*" in *Camus: A Collection of Critical Essays,* ed. Germaine Brée (Englewood Cliffs, N.J.: Prentice-Hall, 1962), p. 110.
8. Gen. 4:16.
9. Jacques Ellul, *The Meaning of the City* (Grand Rapids: Wm. B. Eerdmans Publishing Co., 1970), p. 1.
10. Yevgeny Yevtushenko, "Being Famous Isn't Pretty," *Harper's Magazine,* July 1971, p. 57.
11. Reidar Thomte, *Kierkegaard's Philosophy of Religion* (Princeton, N.J.: Princeton University Press, 1948), pp. 167, 169.
12. Edward V. Stein, *Guilt: Theory and Therapy* (Philadelphia: The Westminster Press, 1968), p. 166.
13. Gen. 4:14.
14. Gen. 4:15b.
15. Ernest T. Campbell, "Afraid to Be Free," *The Pulpit,* Vol. XL, No. 8 (Sept. 1969), p. 6.

The Adventure of Hope
1. Heb. 11:8-10.
2. Luke 16:19-24.
3. Gen. 12:11-13.
4. Gen. 12:18-19.
5. Gen. 23:1-2.
6. Gen. 13:9-10, 12.
7. Gen. 18:20-21, 23-26.
8. Quoted in Samuel Marinus Zwemer, *Sons of Adam* (Grand Rapids: Baker Book House, 1951), pp. 46-47.
9. Immanuel Kant, *Critique of Pure Reason* (London: J. M. Dent & Sons, 1934), p. 457.
10. "The Laity, Man in One and Many Worlds," by the Department on the Laity of the World Council of Churches, in *Dead or Alive,* 41st Annual Report, 1966, Board of Evangelism and Social Service, United Church of Canada, p. 126.
11. Heb. 11:8.

Past the Breaking Places
1. Gen. 19:1-2, 12-13, 15, 17, 24-26.
2. Kurt Vonnegut, Jr., *Slaughterhouse-Five* (London: Grenada Publishers, 1972), p. 21.

3. Dorothy Leiser, "Lot's Wife." Copyright 1971 Christian Century Foundation. Reprinted by permission from the September 29, 1971, issue of *The Christian Century*.

4. Eugen Rosenstock-Huessy, *The Christian Future* (New York: Harper & Row, 1966), p. 168.

5. Hank Ketcham, *Dennis the Menace* (New York: Henry Holt and Co., 1952), back cover.

6. John Updike, *Rabbit Redux* (New York: Alfred A. Knopf, 1971), p. 78.

7. T. S. Eliot, "East Coker," in *Four Quartets* (New York: Harcourt Brace Jovanovich, 1943), p. 17. Used by permission.

8. Luke 17:31-32.

9. W. H. Bennett, ed., *Genesis,* Vol. I, *The New-Century Bible* (New York: Oxford University Press, n.d.), p. 221.

10. *Ibid.,* p. 222.

Story of a Stranger in the Night

1. Gen. 32:24-31.

2. Frederick Buechner, *The Magnificent Defeat* (New York: The Seabury Press, 1966), p. 11.

3. W. Robertson Smith, *Religion of the Semites* (London: Adam and Charles Black, 1901), p. 380.

4. Walt Whitman, *Leaves of Grass* (New York: Books, Inc., n.d.), p. 29.

5. Harry Emerson Fosdick, *What Is Vital in Religion* (New York: Harper & Brothers, 1955), p. 9.

6. Gen. 33:4.

Holding Things Together

1. Gen. 32:24-31.

2. Gen. 21:6, N.E.B.

3. Heb. 11:4-11, 20.

4. Gen. 24:1-4.

5. Gen. 25:27-28.

6. Gen. 26:16-22.

7. Gen. 26:23-24.

8. Gen. 26:26-31.

9. T. S. Settel, ed., *The Light and the Rock: The Vision of Dag Hammarskjöld* (New York: E. P. Dutton & Co., 1966), p. 26.

10. Heb. 11:20.

11. Viktor E. Frankl, *Man's Search for Meaning* (New York: Washington Square Press, 1963), p. 169.

12. Lloyd C. Douglas, *The Living Faith* (Boston: Houghton Mifflin Company, 1955), p. 140.

The Problems of Ordinary People
1. W. O. E. Oesterley and Theodore H. Robinson, *Hebrew Religion: Its Origin and Development* (New York: The Macmillan Co., 1930), p. 134.
2. Exod. 1:22—2:8, 10.
3. Exod. 2:11-12.
4. Exod. 3:1-6.
5. Exod. 3:13-14.
6. James Joyce, *Ulysses* (New York: Random House, Vintage Books, 1914), p. 213.
7. Exod. 3:7-10.
8. Deut. 32:48-50, 52; 34:1-8, 10-12.
9. Marc Connelly, *The Green Pastures* (New York: Rinehart & Co., 1929), pp. 144, 147.
10. *New Songs of Inspiration, No. 3* (Nashville: John T. Benson Publishing Co., 1958), p. 72.

So There Are Giants Ahead
1. Joshua 1:1-6.
2. Joshua 6:20-21.
3. Fleming James, *Personalities of the Old Testament* (New York: Charles Scribner's Sons, 1939), p. 51.
4. Joshua 24:1-4, 6, 14-15, 29.
5. *The Interpreter's Bible,* Vol. II, p. 552.
6. Num. 13:17-21, 23, 25-29.
7. Num. 13:30-33.
8. Num. 14:7-9.
9. Settel, *op cit.,* p. 44.

The King Arthur of Jewish History
1. 2 Sam. 7:16.
2. 1 Sam. 16:17-19, 21, 23.
3. 1 Sam. 17:4-11.
4. 1 Sam. 17:31-37.
5. 1 Sam. 18:6-9.
6. James, *op. cit.,* p. 124.
7. 1 Sam. 27:9.
8. 1 Sam. 27:11b-12a.
9. 2 Sam. 18:33.
10. 2 Sam. 12:1-7, 13.
11. Acts 13:22.
12. 2 Sam. 1:19-20.
13. 2 Sam. 1:25-26.
14. 1 Peter 4:8b.
15. Luke 7:47.

16. Ps. 51:1-2.

17. Lynn Harold Hough, *The Meaning of Human Experience* (Nashville: Abingdon Press, 1945), p. 88.

Protecting Ourselves from the Truth

1. 1 Kings 16:29-30.
2. 1 Kings 22:41-44.
3. 1 Kings 22:4b.
4. 1 Kings 22:5.
5. 1 Kings 22:6.
6. 1 Kings 22:7-8.
7. 1 Kings 22:15.
8. 1 Kings 22:16-18.
9. 1 Kings 22:26-27.
10. 1 Kings 22:37-40.
11. Quoted by William C. Bullitt, "Tragedy of Versailles," *Life,* March 27, 1944, p. 99.
12. Winston S. Churchill, *The Second World War,* Vol. VI, *Triumph and Tragedy* (Boston: Houghton Mifflin Co., 1948).
13. Eda J. LeShan, *How to Survive Parenthood* (New York: Random House, 1965), p. 83.

Wisdom No One Wants

1. George Adam Smith, *The Book of the Twelve Prophets,* Vol. I (New York: Harper & Brothers, n.d.), p. 72.
2. Amos 1:2-3, 6-7, 9.
3. Amos 2:6-7a.
4. Hughell E. W. Fosbroke in *The Interpreter's Bible,* Vol. VI, p. 764.
5. Amos 3:1-2.
6. Amos 4:1-2.
7. Amos 4:4-5.
8. Amos 5:21-24.
9. Amos 7:10, 12-13.
10. Amos 7:14-15.
11. Quoted by Stella Pitts, interview with Murry C. "Jack" Falkner, New Orleans *Times Picayune,* July 9, 1972.
12. Amos 7:7-9.
13. Amos 5:21, 24.
14. Amos 9:7.
15. John Paterson, *The Goodly Fellowship of the Prophets* (New York: Charles Scribner's Sons, 1948), p. 11.
16. Quoted in *Harper's Magazine,* August 1968, p. 24.
17. 1 Cor. 1:25.
18. Amos 5:23-24.

The Pain of Love
   1. Hos. 1:1-3, N.E.B.
   2. Hos. 1:9, N.E.B.
   3. Hos. 2:2-5, N.E.B.
   4. Hos. 2:8, N.E.B.
   5. Hos. 2:11-13, N.E.B.
   6. Edwin Lewis, *The Biblical Faith and Christian Freedom* (Philadelphia: The Westminster Press, 1953), p. 136.
   7. Hos. 3:2-3, N.E.B.
   8. George Adam Smith, *op. cit.,* p. 85.
   9. Alan Paton, *Too Late the Phalarope* (New York: Charles Scribner's Sons, 1953), pp. 250, 252-253.
   10. *Ibid.,* p. 265.
   11. Hos. 2:14, N.E.B.
   12. Hos. 2:16, N.E.B.
   13. George Adam Smith, *op. cit.,* p. 262.
   14. Hos. 11:1-4.
   15. Hos. 11:8-9.
   16. Ps. 139:8.
   17. Hos. 14:4-7.

The Sleep of the Innocent
   1. Jonah 1:2-3, N.E.B.
   2. Jonah 1:4, N.E.B.
   3. Jonah 1:14, N.E.B.
   4. Jonah 2:10—3:1, N.E.B.
   5. Jonah 3:3, N.E.B.
   6. Jonah 3:6, N.E.B.
   7. Jonah 3:10, N.E.B.
   8. Jonah 4:1-3, N.E.B.
   9. Carl Knopf, *The Old Testament Speaks* (New York: Thomas Nelson & Sons, 1933), p. 334.
   10. Jonah 4:10-11, N.E.B.

The Frailty of a Blameless Man
   1. Job 1:1-3, N.E.B.
   2. Job 1:20-22, N.E.B.
   3. Job 3:20, 23; 6:11-13; 7:17-19; 10:18a; 21:7, 15, N.E.B.
   4. Job 1:1, N.E.B.
   5. Job 27:2-6, N.E.B.
   6. Clark Hunt, *Mighty Men of God* (Nashville: Abingdon Press, 1959), p. 87.
   7. Job 3:1-7, 26; 7:11, 16; 10:1-2; 14:1-2; 19:7-8a, N.E.B.
   8. Archibald MacLeish, *J.B.* (Boston: Houghton Mifflin Co., 1958), p. 135. Used by permission.

9. Job 31:35, 37, N.E.B.
10. Richard B. Sewall, *The Vision of Tragedy* (New Haven, Conn.: Yale University Press, 1959), p. 22.
11. Thomas Wolfe, "God's Lonely Man," in *The Hills Beyond* (New York: Harper & Brothers, 1941), p. 190.
12. Job 2:9-10, N.E.B.
13. H. Wheeler Robinson, *The Cross in the Old Testament* (Philadelphia: The Westminster Press, 1955), p. 16.
14. Job 2:11-13, N.E.B.
15. Alexander Pope, *Thoughts on Various Subjects*.
16. Samuel Terrien, *Job: Poet of Existence* (New York: The Bobbs-Merrill Co., 1957), p. 69.
17. Job 38:2-3, N.E.B.
18. Job 42:5.
19. MacLeish, *op. cit.*, pp. 12, 13.

Epilogue
1. Acts 9:1-8; 22:3-21; 26:4-23.
2. Phil. 3:4-6.
3. Rom. 3:10.
4. Dietrich Bonhoeffer, *Letters and Papers from Prison* (New York: The Macmillan Co., Paperbacks Edition, 1962), p. 226.
5. Rom. 7:24-25.
6. 1 Cor. 15:57.